Cartography
MALCOLM PORTER

Editor
MICHAEL COOPER

Text
KEITH LYE
DAVID ROSS

Illustrations
MIKE ATKINSON
MIKE SAUNDERS

Published by Granada Publishing 1985
Granada Publishing Limited
8 Grafton Street, London W1X 3LA

Copyright © Granada Publishing 1985

Material in the Our World and Flags section of this book
has previously been published in the Granada Guide to
Flags 1981 and to Planet Earth 1983.

British Library Cataloguing in Publication Data
Cooper, Michael
    The new children's atlas.
    1. Atlases – Juvenile literature
    I. Title
    912   G1021

ISBN 0-246-12788-0

Printed in Great Britain by
Purnell & Sons

MICHAEL COOPER

The New Children's Atlas

GRANADA

Our World ... 8–17

An introduction to the planet Earth, its position and movement in space, its measurement, its formation and structure, its climate; the drifting of its continents – and the changes wrought by rivers, winds, ice, oceans – and man.

Flags ...

The flags of nations and states are illustrated with a description of their origins, development

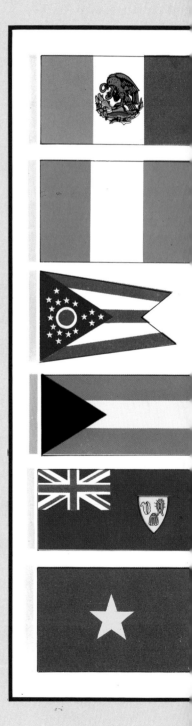

and symbolism. The populations and sizes of the countries are also given.

Original world maps showing geological features as well as country boundaries and towns, together with a comprehensive index. In addition there is an index to Our World and to Flags.

OUR WORLD

The Earth is one of nine planets that rotate around the Sun in the Solar System. The Earth is only a tiny speck in space. The Sun's diameter is 109 times that of the Earth. And the Sun is only a medium-sized star, one of about 100,000 in the Milky Way galaxy. Some of these stars may have planets much like our Earth orbiting around them.

The Earth is a terrestrial planet – that is, it is dense and rocky, like Mars, Mercury, Pluto and Venus. Jupiter, Neptune, Saturn and Uranus are much larger, low-density balls of gas.

People once thought that the Earth was flat. But photographs taken from space show that it is round. It is not a perfect sphere. It bulges out slightly at the equator and is flattened at the poles. The polar diameter, joining the North and South poles via the

centre of the Earth is 12,713 km long. The diameter across the equator is 43 km longer.

The Earth looks blue from space, because water covers about 71 per cent of the planet's surface. Water is one of the three parts of the Earth. It is called the *hydrosphere*. The other parts are the *lithosphere* (the rocks) and the *atmosphere* (the air around the Earth). The Earth is forever changing. The oceans are being widened or made smaller by movements in the rocks under the Earth's crust. The lithosphere changes as volcanoes create new rocks and surface rocks are worn away. The atmosphere is always on the move, making the weather change from day to day. Life on Earth has also changed throughout a 4600 million-year-long history.

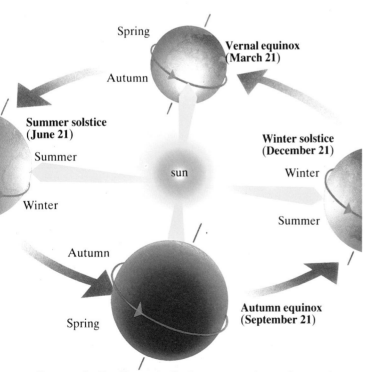

Because the Earth's axis is tilted, sometimes the northern and sometimes the southern hemisphere leans towards the Sun. The seasons in the two hemispheres are opposite to each other.

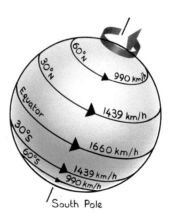

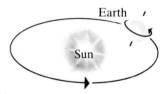

Above: The Earth takes about 365¼ days to make one complete journey around the Sun. Left: The Earth spins like a top once every 24 hours. The speed at which the Earth rotates decreases away from the equator.

Earth Time

The Earth is racing through space in three ways. First, the entire Solar System is swinging around the centre of the Milky Way galaxy at a speed of 69,200 km/h. Second, the Earth rotates around the Sun at an average speed of 106,200 km/h, taking one *solar year* (365 days, 5 hours, 48 minutes and 46 seconds) to complete the journey. A solar year is about one-fourth of a day more than the calendar year of 365 days. This extra time is allowed for on calendars

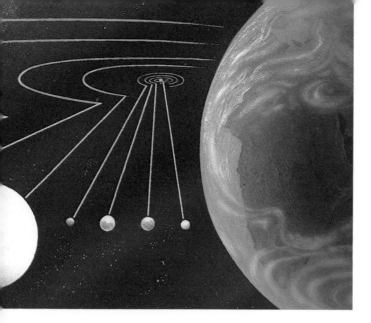

The planets of the Solar System (from left to right):
Pluto, Neptune, Uranus, Saturn, Jupiter, Mars, Earth,
Venus and Mercury. Right: The Earth as seen from space.

by having a leap year of 366 days every four years. The Earth also spins on its axis in one *mean solar day* (24 hours). The axis is the imaginary line joining the North and South poles. As the Earth spins, the Sun appears to move across the sky from the east, where it rises, to the west, where it sets.

Because the Earth's axis is tilted by 23½°, the northern and southern hemispheres experience seasons. On March 21, the *vernal equinox*, the Sun is overhead at the equator and its heat is evenly distributed. But after March 21, as the Earth rotates, the northern hemisphere starts to tilt towards the Sun. On June 21, the *summer solstice*, the Sun is overhead at the Tropic of Cancer (latitude 23½° North) and the northern hemisphere gets more heat than the southern. After June 21, the northern hemisphere gradually tilts away from the Sun. On September 23, the *autumn equinox*, the Sun is overhead at the equator. The southern hemisphere then tilts towards the Sun. On December 21, the *winter solstice*, the Sun is overhead at the Tropic of Capricorn (23½° South), where it is summer.

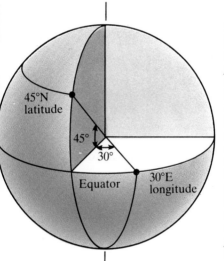

Lines of latitude are imaginary lines around the Earth that are parallel to the equator, which is 0°. The North Pole is latitude 90° North and the South Pole is 90° South. The latitude of any other point is the angle formed at the centre of the Earth between the point and the equator. Lines of longitude, or meridians, are measured either 180° east, or 180° west of the prime meridian, which is 0° longitude.

Measuring the Earth

The position of any place on Earth is described by two measurements, latitude and longitude. Lines of latitude and longitude appear on maps, which show part or all of the Earth's surface on a flat piece of paper. The latitude of a place is a measurement of how far it is north or south of the equator – that is, between 0° latitude (the equator) and 90° North (the North Pole) or 90° South (the South Pole). The distance from the equator to one of the poles is about 10,002 km, so 1° of latitude is 111 km.

The longitude of a place is a measurement of how far the place is east or west of the prime meridian, or 0° longitude. The prime meridian runs from the North Pole to the South Pole through the former Royal Astronomical Observatory at Greenwich, London. At the equator, 1° of longitude is 111 km. At the poles, it is zero, because all the lines meet there.

The line of longitude 180° West is the same as 180° East. This line of longitude is the International Date Line. If you travel from east to west across this line, you lose a whole day. But if you travel from west to east, you gain a day. This happens because 15° of longitude represent one hour of time as the Earth spins on its axis. Hence, if you travel east of Greenwich, you must advance your clock by one hour for every 15° of longitude, so that at 180° East, the time is 12 hours *ahead* of Greenwich. Travelling west, you put your clock back by one hour for every 15° of longitude. Hence, at 180° West, the time is 12 hours *behind* Greenwich. This means that the time difference between two points on either side of the International Date Line is 24 hours.

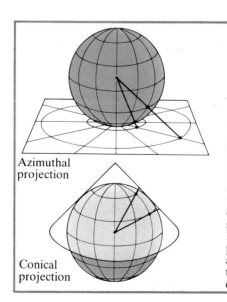

MAP PROJECTIONS Curved surfaces cannot be shown accurately on a flat map. Perspective map projections are made by imagining the Earth as a glass globe with a light at its centre. Shadows of lines of latitude and longitude are cast onto paper, as in the azimuthal and conical projections shown here. Perspective map projections are often adjusted to reduce the amount of distortion.

Azimuthal projection

Conical projection

Formation of the Earth

Scientists have put forward several theories to explain the origin of the Solar System. Some think that it was formed from material pulled away from the Sun when a star passed near it. Others consider that the Sun was once extremely large. As it spun around, it threw out gases and dust into a disc. This material formed into planets. But most scientists think that the Solar System formed from a huge cloud of dust and gas, the remains of exploded stars. Material in this cloud was drawn by gravity to the centre to form the Sun. The rest of the material was drawn into blobs around 4600 million years ago. These blobs developed into planets.

The new-born Earth was fiercely hot. Heavy substances sank towards the centre of the molten body. Lighter substances were thrown upwards by volcanic explosions which released gases and water vapour from the rocks. The water vapour formed clouds and heavy rain lashed the blazing surface. Slowly, the surface hardened to form a thin crust. Occasionally, molten rocks burst through the crust in volcanoes.

The Earth is now divided into three main zones: the crust, mantle and core. The crust reaches a maximum depth of 60–70 km under mountain ranges. The oceanic crust, however, is only about 6 km thick. The crust consists mostly of light materials. It rests upon the mostly solid, 2900-km-thick mantle, where the rocks are much denser (heavier). The densest zone, however, is the core, which has a diameter of about 6920 km. The outer part of the core is probably molten, and the inner core solid.

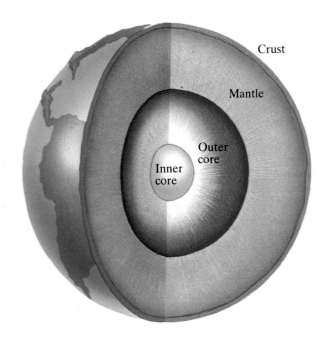

The Earth is covered by a hard, thin crust. Beneath the crust is the thick, dense mantle. The Earth's core is divided into a liquid outer core and a solid inner core.

Igneous Rocks

Minerals are homogeneous substances. This means that they have a definite chemical composition and that any part of a mineral is exactly the same as any other part. Rocks consist of minerals, but the amounts of minerals in a rock vary from one sample to another. This means that rocks do not have a definite chemical composition.

There are three main kinds of rocks: igneous rocks, sedimentary rocks and metamorphic rocks. Igneous rocks are formed from magma. Magma is molten rock that has risen up through the Earth's crust.

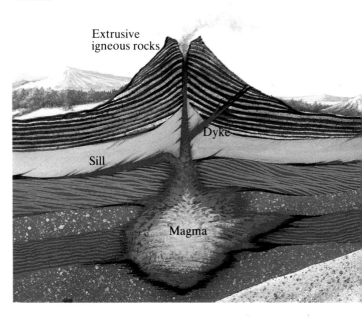

Igneous rocks form in several ways. The common rock basalt is hardened lava. Granite forms from molten rock that has hardened well below the surface. Obsidian, or volcanic glass, forms on the surface from magma that cools rapidly in the air.

Sedimentary and Metamorphic Rocks

Many sedimentary rocks are made up of worn fragments of rock. These fragments, including pebbles, sand and mud, are swept into lakes and seas by rivers. There they pile up in layers. The layers, or *strata*, are compressed and the grains of sand and mud are cemented together by minerals deposited by seeping water. Such rocks are called *clastic* rocks. They include conglomerates, sandstones, mudstones and shales.

Metamorphic rocks are igneous or sedimentary rocks that have been changed by great heat, pressure or chemical action. Metamorphic rocks include marble, which was formerly limestone, slate, which was originally shale, mudstone or tuff, and quartzite, which formed from quartz sandstones.

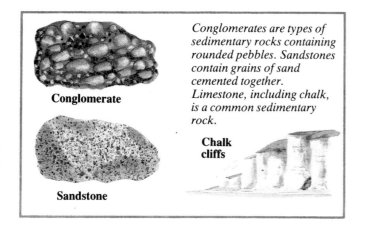

Conglomerates are types of sedimentary rocks containing rounded pebbles. Sandstones contain grains of sand cemented together. Limestone, including chalk, is a common sedimentary rock.

Conglomerate

Sandstone

Chalk cliffs

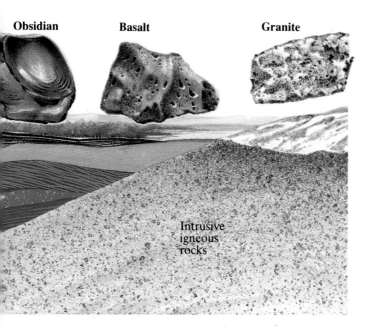

Obsidian　　Basalt　　Granite

Intrusive igneous rocks

Climate and Vegetation

Climate is the average, or usual, weather of a place. It is based mainly on average temperatures and rainfall. One major factor affecting climate is latitude – that is, how near the place is to the tropics or polar regions. But other factors, such as the height of the land, are important. Snow-capped mountain peaks on the equator have a polar climate. Nearness to the sea also affects climate. For example, northern Norway is within the Arctic Circle, but its coasts are warmed by an ocean current that flows across the Atlantic Ocean from the Caribbean Sea. By contrast, places at the hearts of continents have severe climates.

There are several types of climate. Tropical climates include hot and wet equatorial regions, with rain all the year round. This climate supports dense forests, like those in the Amazon and Zaire basins. Around the forests are hot areas with a marked dry season. These areas contain light forests or savanna (grassland). The savanna merges in parts of the horse latitude zones into hot deserts.

Temperate zones range from Mediterranean lands with hot, dry summers and cool, moist winters, to the cool coniferous forest regions of the northern hemisphere. Beyond the coniferous forests is the treeless tundra with its long winters. And beyond the tundra are the snow-covered polar lands.

The climate determines the vegetation and animal life of a region. But people can live comfortably anywhere, if their homes are equipped with central heating and air conditioning.

Other sedimentary rocks are of organic origin. Organic rocks consist mostly of the remains of once-living things. For example, coal consists of the remains of ancient swamp plants and some limestones are composed of the shells of sea creatures.

Many sedimentary rocks form in seas from material worn from the land. Rivers transport the sediment to the sea.

Sand and pebbles

Sand

Mud

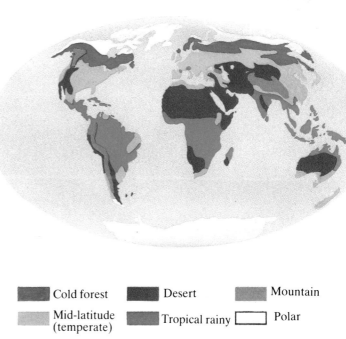

■ Cold forest	■ Desert	■ Mountain
■ Mid-latitude (temperate)	■ Tropical rainy	□ Polar

The Oceans

A better name for our planet would be 'Water' or 'Ocean', because oceans cover 71 per cent of the globe. Until recently, little was known about the world beneath the waves, but in the last 30 to 40 years, the study of the oceans has become a major science. Large parts of the oceans have been mapped and scientists have visited the deepest parts of the oceans in vessels called bathyscaphes and bathyspheres. We now realize that the oceans are a great storehouse of food and minerals for the future.

Left: If you look at a globe, you will find views that include most of the world's land masses, such as the view shown below. But another view is dominated by the largest of the oceans, the Pacific. This view is sometimes called the water hemisphere. The oceans cover about 71 per cent of the Earth's surface.

The oceans are divided into three main zones: the continental shelves, the continental slopes, and the abyss. The continental shelves are gently sloping areas near the continents. Some continental shelves, such as that off western Europe, extend far out to sea. Others, such as that off the western coast of South America, are narrow. The shelves end at the continental slopes, which plunge sharply down to the abyss. The top of the continental slope is the true edge of the continental land masses.

The abyss contains plains, long mountain ranges, called oceanic ridges, and volcanic mountains, some of which form islands. The volcano Mauna Kea, in Hawaii, can claim to be the world's highest mountain. It rises 10,023 metres from the ocean floor, although only 4204 metres are above sea level. The average depth of the oceans is about 3550 metres, but the ocean trenches are much deeper. A record depth of 11,033 metres has been measured in the Marianas Trench in the Pacific Ocean.

The oceans are youthful features in geological terms. Although rocks more than 3500 million years old have been found on land, no rocks on the ocean bed are more than 200 million years old.

The oceans are interconnected and contain nearly 1300 million cubic kilometres of water. This is more than 97 per cent of the world's water. Most of the remainder is locked in ice sheets.

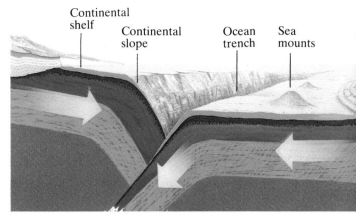

Continental shelf · Continental slope · Ocean trench · Sea mounts

The ocean bed has varied scenery, with volcanic mountains and islands, ocean trenches, plains, mountain ranges and canyons.

The Changing Earth

In one person's lifetime, the land may not appear to change much. In fact, it is changing all the time. Some changes are dramatic, as when Mount St Helens erupted in the USA in 1980, killing 65 people in an explosion that ripped about 425 metres from the top of the volcano. Most changes, however, are slow. They include the natural erosion of the land and the slow drifting of the continents.

Continents have been on the move for millions of years. But the theory of continental drift has been accepted by most scientists for barely 20 years. Evidence for continental drift can be seen on a world map, where North and South America look as though they would fit against Europe and Africa like pieces in a giant jigsaw. The fit is even better if, instead of the coasts, the edges of the continental shelves, the true edges of the continents, are placed together. Other evidence for drift comes from the studies of rocks and fossils.

Scientists now believe that, 200 million years ago, there was only one continent. They call this continent Pangaea. Pangaea gradually broke apart and the continents slowly moved, at rates between one and ten centimetres a year, to their present positions. Continental drift continues today. For example, the Atlantic Ocean is still getting wider, while the Mediterranean Sea is closing up.

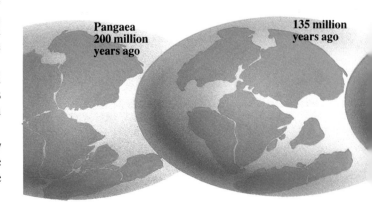

Pangaea 200 million years ago · 135 million years ago

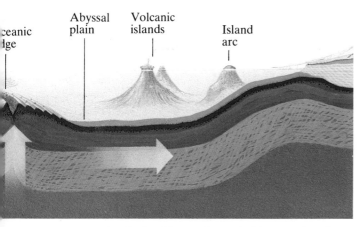

The Earth's crust is split into large, rigid sections called *tectonic plates*. These consist of continents, continental shelves and the ocean crust that also underlies the continents. The plates rest on the dense mantle. In the upper mantle, heat causes semi-fluid rock to rise. Just beneath the plates, the rocks spread outwards until, finally, they cool and sink. These movements are called *convection currents*. They occur directly under the ocean ridges, which are plate edges. As the hot rocks rise and spread outwards, they pull the plates along with them. Hot magma plugs the gap as the plates move apart and then cools to become crustal rock.

The map shows that the Earth's crust is cracked into a series of plates, both large and small. These plates are continually moving.

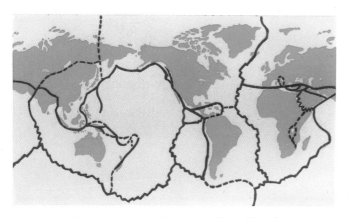

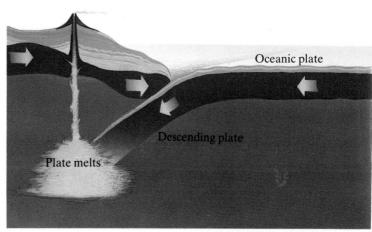

Ocean spreading occurs along the ocean ridges. The plates on either side of the ridges are pulled apart by convection currents in the upper mantle. The gaps are filled by volcanic rock.

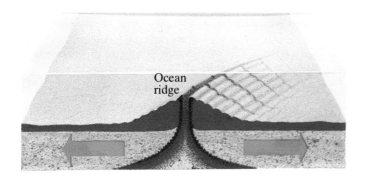

When two plates push against each other, one slides down beneath the other. As it descends, the edge of the plate melts. The melted rock, or magma, may rise to the Earth's surface through volcanoes.

Right: Some plates slide past each other. The plate boundary is a transform fault. The San Andreas Fault in California is a plate edge of this type.

These maps show how the oceans formed as the continents drifted apart in the last 200 million years. The continents were formerly joined in a super-continent called Pangaea.

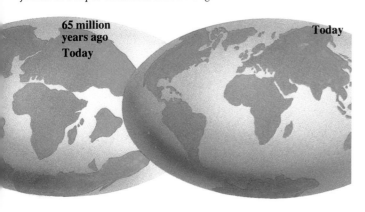

New crustal rock is, therefore, being created along the ocean ridges. Elsewhere, crustal rock is being destroyed. The destruction takes place under the deep ocean trenches where one plate is forced down beneath another. As the plate descends, friction, pressure and heat melt the edge of the plate. This creates magma, which may then rise through volcanoes in the overlying plate.

Ocean ridges and trenches are two of the three kinds of plate edges. The third is the transform fault. Along these faults (cracks), the plates move jerkily alongside each other. Plate edges are associated with earthquakes and volcanic activity. The study of plate movements has helped geologists to explain how these phenomena occur.

13

Earthquakes

Earthquakes are caused by shock waves that travel through the Earth's crust. They may be generated by landslides, explosions or volcanic eruptions, but most result from sudden movements along faults in the rocks. Earthquakes can occur anywhere, although the most destructive ones strike near plate edges.

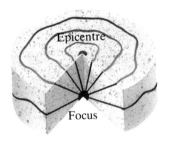

Left: The focus is the place where an earthquake originates. The point on the surface above the focus is the epicentre. Isoseismal lines join points with the same degree of shock.

Plate movements are never smooth. For example, the plate edges along transform faults become jammed. The pressure slowly mounts over a number of years. Suddenly the jammed rocks snap and the plates jerk forward, triggering off an earthquake.

An average of 10,000 earthquakes are recorded every year. Most of them have a low *magnitude* (strength), but around 10 cause loss of life and destruction of property. In 1556, a record number of about 800,000 people perished in a terrible earthquake in China. Earthquakes may cause fires, started by broken gas pipes and electrical short-circuits. Scientists are still trying to find accurate ways of forecasting earthquakes.

Volcanoes

Volcanoes are the outlets for hot magma from the Earth's interior. Most of the world's 530 or so active volcanoes are situated near plate edges, notably along the ocean ridges and near the *subduction zones*, where one plate is descending beneath another. The descending plate melts and creates a reservoir of magma. Some volcanoes, like those in Hawaii in the central Pacific, lie far from plate edges. The magma here comes from a 'hot spot' in the mantle, where magma is probably created by radioactive heat.

Some volcanoes are explosive. When they erupt, they explode clouds of hot ash and gases into the air. Other volcanoes are quiet. There are no massive explosions when they erupt. Instead, runny lava gushes out of the volcano's *vent* (opening) and builds up low, *shield* volcanoes. Most volcanoes are intermediate in type, sometimes erupting explosively and sometimes quietly. Intermediate volcanoes have *composite* cones, composed of alternating layers of hardened lava and compacted ash.

Scientific stations have been built around active volcanoes in thickly populated areas, such as at

Mount Vesuvius in Italy. Any changes in heat and pressure inside the volcano are carefully watched. And instruments called *tiltometers* measure any changes in the gradient of the sides of a volcano caused by the swelling of magma below. The scientists issue warnings when they think an eruption is likely.

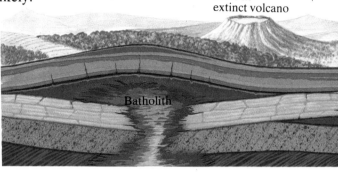

Lake in extinct volcano

Batholith

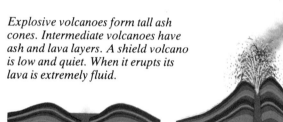

Explosive volcanoes form tall ash cones. Intermediate volcanoes have ash and lava layers. A shield volcano is low and quiet. When it erupts its lava is extremely fluid.

Mountain Building

The three main kinds of mountains are volcanoes fold mountains and block mountains.

Fold mountains are formed by enormous lateral (sideways) pressure. This pressure twists and buckles formerly flat rock layers into loops, called *folds*. A simple upfold is called an *anticline*, and a downfold is a *syncline*. An *anticlinorium* is a large anticline, containing within it many small anticlines. Sometimes, folds are turned on their sides. These are called *recumbent* folds. Sometimes, folds are broken away and pushed many kilometres over other rocks; such folds are called *nappes*.

How then did the world's highest fold mountains, the Himalayas in northern India, form? About 200 million years ago, the Indian land mass was joined to Africa and Antarctica.

Around 180 million years ago, this plate began to

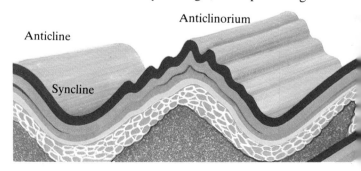

Anticlinorium

Anticline

Syncline

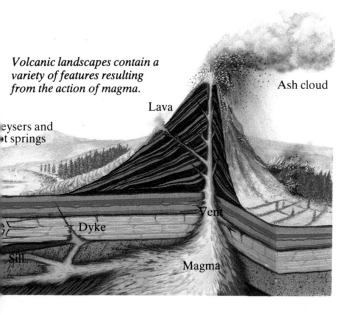

Volcanic landscapes contain a variety of features resulting from the action of magma.

Ash cloud

Lava

Geysers and hot springs

Vent

Dyke

Sill

Magma

Limestone caves are worn out by chemical weathering. They are dissolved by rainwater which has dissolved carbon dioxide from the air and the soil, so becoming a weak acid.

drift away. By about 50 million years ago, it was pushing against the huge Asian plate. The rocks on the sea bed between the two plates were squeezed together. They slowly rose up to form the Himalayan range. Today, the Indian and Asian plates are firmly joined together. The lofty Himalayas are mostly formed from sedimentary rocks that piled up in a sea that no longer exists. Fossils of sea creatures have been found near the top of Mount Everest, the highest peak in the Himalayas.

Other fold mountains include the Alps in Europe. They began to rise about 26 million years ago when a plate bearing Italy pushed against the European plate. Other major fold mountains include the Andes in South America and the Rockies in North America.

Block mountains, or *horsts*, are blocks of land that were squeezed up between long faults in the Earth's crust. Blocks of land also sank between faults to form steep-sided rift valleys, or *graben*. Like fold mountains, these features are caused by plate movements. Examples of block mountains include the Ruwenzori range which overlooks the deep East African Rift Valley. In Europe, the Vosges Mountains and the Black Forest are block mountains bordering a rift valley that contains the River Rhine.

Great sideways pressure squeezes rocks into anticlines, synclines, complex anticlinoriums and nappes. Fold mountains are formed when two plates are pushed against each other. Block mountains and rift valleys form between parallel sets of faults.

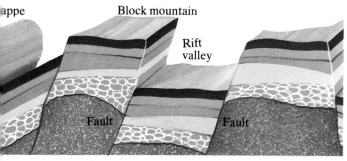

Nappe

Block mountain

Rift valley

Fault

Fault

Weathering

Even as mountain ranges are being formed, natural forces wear them down. Natural erosion continues all the time. On average, a depth of about 3.5 cm of land is stripped off all land surfaces every 1000 years.

One group of natural forces is called weathering. Mechanical weathering includes frost action, which occurs because ice takes up over nine per cent more space that the water from which it formed. Hence, when water freezes in the cracks in rocks the ice exerts pressure. It widens the cracks until bits of rock break away. In mountain areas, the rock fragments pile up in huge heaps called scree or talus. In hot deserts, intense heating and rapid cooling make the outer layers of rocks peel away. Mechanical weathering also includes the action of plants and burrowing animals, which break up rocks. An example of

Rocks shattered by frost action in rainy mountain areas pile up in heaps called scree.

Rivers

Rivers are important in eroding the land. The Mississippi River alone sweeps more than 700 million tonnes of sediment into the sea every year.

Rivers rise in springs, lakes or in melting glaciers. Youthful rivers usually have a small volume, but when they are swollen by heavy rain or melting snow, they become torrents. They sweep loose rocks downstream and this material wears out more rocks from the river bed. In this way, youthful rivers carve out deep V-shaped valleys. When they reach gentler slopes, the rivers enter maturity. They occupy broader valleys, and often contain sweeping curves called *meanders*. Tributary rivers increase their volume so that they can carry a large load of sediment, while still wearing out their valleys.

In old age, the volume of water is great, but the rivers are sluggish as they cross nearly flat plains. Muddy from their load, they often flood and spread sediment over the plains. The largest particles are dropped first on the river banks, building up mounds called *levees*. Old age rivers may change course and former meanders become swampy *oxbow lakes*.

The rivers finally discharge into the sea. If there are no strong offshore currents, the sediment may accumulate in new land areas called *deltas*. Otherwise, it is swept out to sea where it piles up on the sea bed to form sedimentary rocks.

The Work of Ice

About two per cent of the world's water is locked in ice sheets, ice caps and valley glaciers. Moving ice can cut deeply into the land. Rocks frozen in the bottom and sides of the ice give it the power of a giant file. Glaciers form in mountain basins from compacted snow. The ice spills out of the basins and flows downhill along valleys. Most glaciers flow only about one metre a day. But the speed increases if heavy snowfall or avalanches pile up snow on the glacier's source. Glaciers carry huge loads of frost-shattered rocks called *moraine*. This is either on the surface or frozen in the ice.

Ice wears out distinctive features. Much glaciated scenery exists in the northern hemisphere in areas now free from ice. This land was under the grip of an Ice Age only 10,000 to 20,000 years ago.

In mountains, the basins, or *cirques*, in which glaciers form, are steep-sided. They often contain small lakes called *tarns* after the ice has gone. Cirques are separated from each other by knife-edged ridges called *arêtes*. And if three or more cirques are back to back, the ice carves out a pointed peak, called a *horn*. The most obvious features of all are steep-sided, U-shaped valleys, quite unlike the V-shaped river valleys. Other glacial features are formed from moraine. This eroded material, ranging from boulders to clay, forms low hills, winding ridges and clusters of hummocks.

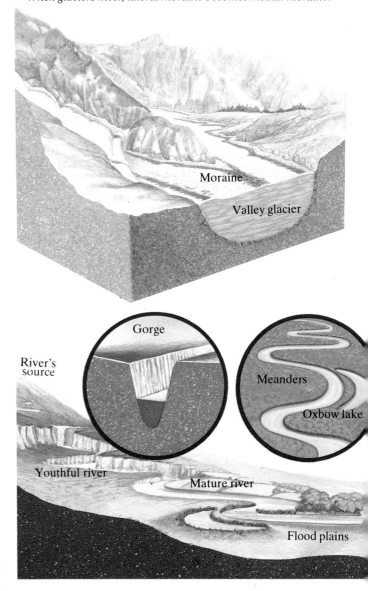

Valley glaciers in mountain regions transport moraine (loose rock). Moraine on the glacier's sides is called lateral moraine. When glaciers meet, lateral moraine becomes medial moraine.

Moraine

Valley glacier

River's source

Gorge

Meanders

Oxbow lake

Youthful river

Mature river

Flood plains

The Work of the Wind

Hot deserts occur in all continents except Europe. Although the average rainfall is low, much desert scenery has been shaped by running water. This may have occurred in the past when the climate was much wetter than it is today. Or it may be caused by occasional storms. The rain may be so intense that large areas are flooded and torrents wear out gullies called *wadis*. Finally, the water sinks into the ground or is evaporated by the Sun.

Normally, the wind is the chief agent of erosion in deserts. Winds carry dust high into the air and lift sand grains a metre or so above the ground. Wind-blown sand moves by bouncing on the surface. As it moves, it polishes and undercuts rocks, scours the ground to create hollows, strips the paint off cars, and cuts right through wooden telegraph poles.

Vast seas of sand, called by an Arabic word *erg*, cover about one-fifth of the hot deserts.

Coasts

While weathering, rivers and ice mould the scenery of inland areas, the sea is the great sculptor of coasts. Waves pound the shore and, in severe storms, they have moved blocks of concrete of 1000 tonnes or more. In storms, waves are armed with stones which they lift up and hurl at cliffs. This bombardment wears out caves at the base of cliffs. Finally, the overlying rocks are dislodged and crash down. Waves also trap and compress air in cracks and holes in rocks. When the pressure is released, the air expands explosively, enlarging cracks or shattering the rocks. The sea dissolves some rocks. It also churns loose rocks together until they become smooth pebbles. Many years of continual churning reduces the pebbles to sand.

Waves erode soft rocks to create bays. Headlands between bays are made up of harder rocks which have

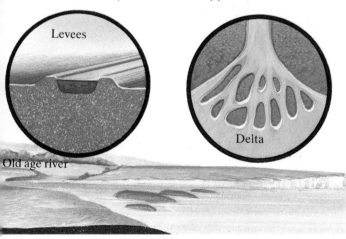

Youthful rivers flow swiftly through deep valleys in their upper courses. Mature rivers develop large meanders and some old age rivers are enclosed by levees. Deltas may form at the river mouth.

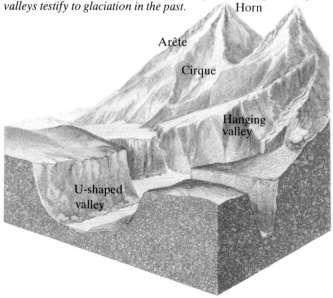

When mountains are freed of snow and ice, such features as pyramidal peaks, knife-edged ridges, cirques and deep, U-shaped valleys testify to glaciation in the past.

Blow-hole

Stack

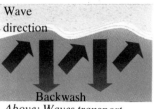

Wave direction

Backwash

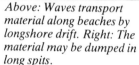

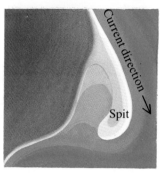

Current direction

Spit

Above: Waves transport material along beaches by longshore drift. Right: The material may be dumped in long spits.

resisted erosion. But even headlands are eventually worn back, as shown in the diagrams at the bottom of this page. Coasts most vulnerable to wave erosion are those made up of loose deposits, such as moraine deposited by glaciers.

Waves and currents transport loose rocks and sand along beaches in a process called *longshore drift*. This is a zig-zag movement which occurs because waves usually sweep diagonally up a beach, pushing loose material along with them. But the backwash always carries the material down at right angles to the beach. Worn material may be swept out to sea, but waves also build new land areas.

Man's Home

About 10,000 years ago, about 8 million people lived on Earth. In the mid-1970s, the world's population passed the 4000 million mark and, by the year 2000, it will probably reach 6000 million. The rapid growth of population is putting a strain on the Earth's resources. For example, increasing amounts of food have been needed, but poor farming methods and overgrazing have caused severe soil erosion. Much farmland has been made infertile and much rich soil has been lost. Nature renews the soil lost by natural erosion. But when the soil is damaged by man-induced soil erosion, it takes a long time before Nature can replace it. There is also a mounting pressure on other resources. Known reserves of oil are likely to run dry in 20 to 30 years time and there may be shortages of many metals.

The factories that produce goods for the world's increasing population have been making Earth a less pleasant place on which to live. Land, sea and air have been polluted by industrial wastes. We are now faced with the challenge of conserving and protecting the Earth's many gifts for unborn generations.

FLAGS

On the following pages the national flags of the countries of the world are shown as they stand as we go to press. As governments change, so do the flags of countries. As you look through the pages you will find there are common features that link countries of similar background, culture and religion. Commonwealth countries sometimes retain a link with the United Kingdom in their flags. In the Arab world the Pan-Arab colours of red, white, black and green will be found, while red, yellow and green are the Pan-African colours often found in that Continent. The flags of Communist countries are red with the star of the Communist Party, while the flags of Christian countries often bear a cross.

Flags of the Americas

United States

Before the start of the War of Independence in 1775, a flag was flown by the Sons of Liberty with nine alternating red and white stripes, standing for the nine colonies that were in revolt against the British. In December of that year the Continental Colours were introduced, with 13 red and white stripes (for the colonies) and the British Union Flag in the canton. In 1777, 13 stars replaced the Union Flag. In 1795 the number of stars and stripes was increased to 15 and the flag became known as the

Star-spangled Banner (above). In 1818 the number of stripes was reduced to 13 and from that time each new state had its own star. The number was most recently increased in 1960 when Hawaii was admitted.

1 Alabama	13 Illinois	27 Nebraska	39 Rhode Island
2 Alaska	14 Indiana	28 Nevada	40 South
3 Arizona	15 Iowa	29 New	Carolina
4 Arkansas	16 Kansas	Hampshire	41 South Dakota
5 California	17 Kentucky	30 New Jersey	42 Tennessee
6 Colorado	18 Louisiana	31 New Mexico	43 Texas
7 Connecticut	19 Maine	32 New York	44 Utah
8 Delaware	20 Maryland	33 North	45 Vermont
* District of	21 Massachusetts	Carolina	46 Virginia
Columbia	22 Michigan	34 North Dakota	47 Washington
9 Florida	23 Minnesota	35 Ohio	48 West Virginia
10 Georgia	24 Mississippi	36 Oklahoma	49 Wisconsin
11 Hawaii	25 Missouri	37 Oregon	50 Wyoming
12 Idaho	26 Montana	38 Pennsylvania	* No number

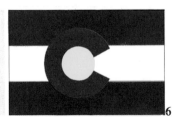

18

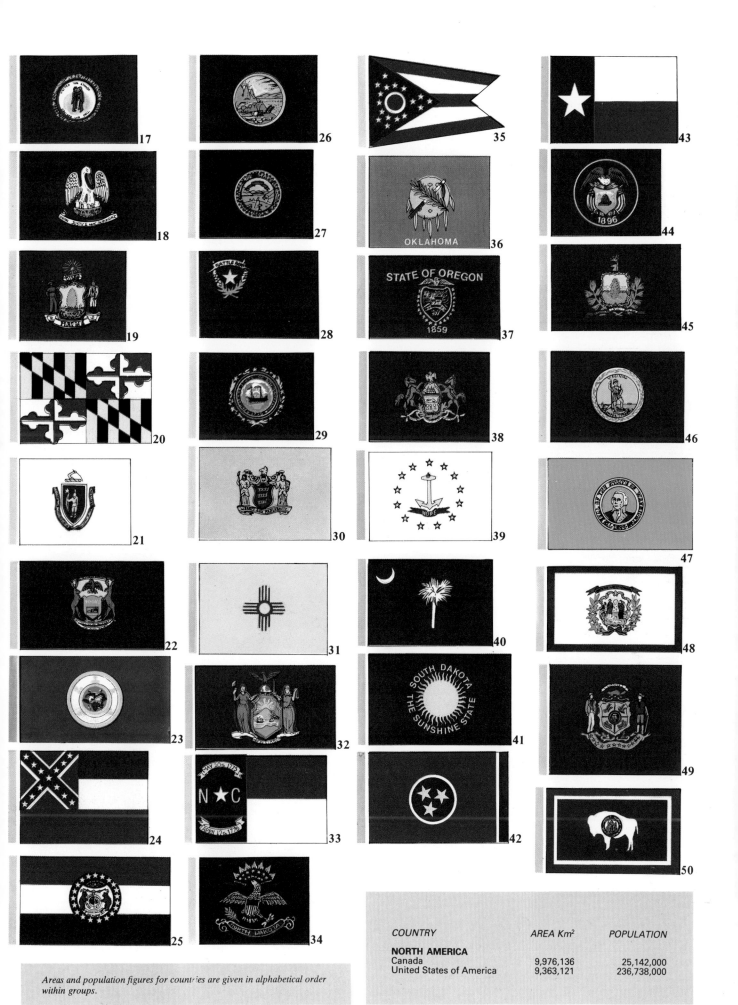

Areas and population figures for countries are given in alphabetical order within groups.

COUNTRY	AREA Km²	POPULATION
NORTH AMERICA		
Canada	9,976,136	25,142,000
United States of America	9,363,121	236,738,000

Canada

The Red Ensign was used from 1892, with the arms in the fly until 1921 when they were replaced with a new shield. Attempts were made to find a more acceptable design, but it was not until 1965 that the present flag was adopted with the maple leaf emblem.

The twelve provinces and territories each have their own flag (adoption dates are shown in brackets):

Alberta (1968)

British Columbia (1960)

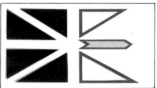

Newfoundland (1979)

Nova Scotia (1929)

Manitoba (1966)

New Brunswick (1965)

North-West Territories (1969)

Prince Edward Island (1964)

Ontario (1965)

Quebec (1948)

Saskatchewan (1969)

The Yukon (1968)

Flags of Central America

Mexico

The present flag was adopted in 1968. The emblem depicts the legendary founding of Mexico City. It shows an eagle, snake and cactus. The colours date back to 1821.

Guatemala

The colours of Central America are used vertically. The present simple design dates from 1971. The state flag shows the national bird of Guatemala, the quetzal, with its long tail feathers. It is a symbol of liberty.

Belize

On full independence from Britain in 1981, Belize added two red stripes to the flag. The coat of arms shows two men, the tools of the country's logging industry and the Latin motto 'I flourish in the shade'.

Honduras

The five stars stand for the original members of the United Provinces of Central America. The flag was officially adopted in 1949.

El Salvador

The traditional Central American colours were adopted in 1912. Two variations are allowed, one bears the motto 'God, Union, Liberty', the other the coat of arms.

Nicaragua

Apart from a slight difference in the shade of blue, Nicaragua's flag is the same as El Salvador's. It dates from 1908, though it is identical to the 1823 United Provinces flag.

Costa Rica

As one of the five states of the United Provinces of Central America, the flag (dating from 1848) retains the blue/white/blue sequence with an additional red stripe.

Panama

The flag dates from Panama's break with Columbia in 1903. Blue is for the Conservatives, red for the Liberals, white for the hope of peace. The red star stands for law and order, the blue star for public honesty.

Flags of South America

Ecuador
Linked until 1830 with Colombia and Venezuela, Ecuador shares with them the flag designed by Francisco de Miranda, under which Simon Bolivar's armies marched.

Colombia
The colours of the flag (see above) represent the nation (yellow), separated by the sea (blue) from Spain whose tyranny the people would resist with their blood (red).

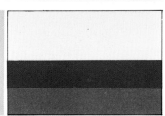

Venezuela
The flag was first used in 1806 when Miranda invaded (see Ecuador). The stars stand for the seven parishes. Only the state flag bears the coat of arms. Private citizens fly the same plain flag as Ecuador.

Guyana
This design was adopted in 1966 on independence. The colours stand for the forests (green), the future (gold), the people's energy (red), their perseverance (black) and the rivers (white).

Surinam
The flag of Surinam, adopted on independence from the Netherlands in 1975, is based on that of the main political parties. The yellow star stands for unity and the nation's golden future.

Guyane
Known in English as French Guiana, Guyane flies the French tricolour. A French possession since 1676, it is now an overseas department of France. Treated as if it were part of the mainland, its citizens elect members to the French parliament.

Peru
General José de San Martin led the liberation of Peru from Spanish rule in 1820 and is said to have chosen red and white as the national colours after a flock of flamingoes flew over his troops.

Brazil
The motto 'Order and Progress' is inscribed on the central sphere. The 23 stars, representing the states and Federal District, are arranged in the pattern of the sky at night as it is seen over Brazil.

Paraguay
Dating from 1842, the flag has the May Star on one side, recalling liberation from Spain in May, 1811, and the State emblem on the reverse.

Bolivia
The colours date from the liberation of 1825. The red stands for the army's valour, yellow for the nation's rich mineral resources, and green for the agricultural wealth of the country.

Uruguay
Flown since 1820 shortly after independence, the blue and white stripes and gold sun are derived from the flag and emblem of Argentina. The original nine provinces are represented in the nine stripes.

Chile
Inspired by the Stars and Stripes of the USA and adopted in the independence struggle in 1817, the white is for the snow on the Andes, blue for the sky and red for the blood of the patriots who died for their country.

Argentina
Blue and white were the colours used in the fight for freedom from Spain. The first flag was raised in 1812. The sun was added to the State flag in 1818.

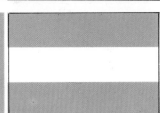

Falkland Islands
This British Dependent Territory flies the Blue Ensign. The sheep on the badge represents the islands' economic mainstay and the ship is the *Desire*, which sailed to discover the islands.

CENTRAL AMERICA		
Belize	22,962	158,000
Costa Rica	50,699	2,589,000
El Salvador	21,393	4,930,000
Guatemala	108,888	8,077,000
Honduras	112,087	4,249,000
Mexico	1,972,546	77,659,000
Nicaragua	129,999	2,934,000
Panama	75,648	2,001,000

SOUTH AMERICA		
Argentina	2,766,889	30,228,000
Bolivia	1,098,579	6,037,000
Brazil	8,511,962	134,380,000
Chile	756,945	11,706,000
Colombia	1,138,913	28,901,000
Ecuador	283,560	8,648,000
Falkland Islands	12,173	3,000
Guyana	214,970	794,000
Guyane	91,000	64,000
Paraguay	406,751	3,623,000
Peru	1,285,214	19,006,000
Surinam	163,265	370,000
Uruguay	176,215	2,926,000
Venezuela	912,050	17,279,000

Flags of the Caribbean

Puerto Rico

A Commonwealth of the United States, the flag is only flown with the Stars and Stripes. The country fought with Cuba for independence from Spain and their flags are almost identical.

Cuba

The 'Lone Star' banner, dating from 1849, was not officially adopted until independence in 1902. The red triangle stands for freedom.

Haiti

The present flag, which started as a variation of the French tricolour, dates from 1964. The two colours represent the country's African heritage.

Dominican Republic

Once a part of Haiti, the Republic's first flag was a white cross over the former blue and red 'French' flag of Haiti. The quarters were rearranged into the present pattern in 1844.

Bahamas

Adopted in 1973, the blue is for the sea that surrounds the 700 islands, the yellow the sands and the black the strength and unity of the people.

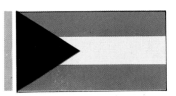

Turks and Caicos Islands

This British Territory flies the Blue Ensign with the coat of arms containing a conch shell, a spiny lobster and a turk's head cactus.

Montserrat

The shield of the Blue Ensign of this British colony dates back to 1909. The Passion cross is held by a female figure in green with a harp.

Cayman Islands

The Blue Ensign is flown by this British Dependent Territory, with the coat of arms, granted in 1958. It shows a turtle and a pineapple.

Bermuda

The Red Ensign with the coat of arms dates from 1915. A red lion holds the wreck of the *Sea Venture* – on which the first settlers sailed in 1609.

British Virgin Islands

A British Dependent Territory, the Blue Ensign carries the islands' badge. It shows a virgin with 12 oil lamps from the Bible story.

Virgin Islands of the United States

The flag of this American Dependency has been flown since 1921. It shows the American eagle with a shield between the letters 'V' and 'I'.

St Christopher-Nevis

These two islands became an Associated State of Great Britain in 1967. The flag has a black palm tree in the central yellow stripe.

Anguilla

Adopted in 1967, the white stands for peace, the blue stripe for hope and youthfulness, the dolphins for strength.

Dominica

Adopted in 1978 on independence, the parrot comes from the arms on the old Blue Ensign. The stars stand for the ten parishes of the island.

Jamaica

Adopted on independence in 1962, the gold stands for the natural resources and sun, green for agriculture and the future, and black for hardships.

St Lucia

The symbol represents the two volcanic formations that rise up from the sea. The island is a former Associated State of Great Britain.

CARIBBEAN		
Anguilla	91	6,000
Antigua	553	80,000
Bahamas	13,934	228,000
Barbados	429	252,000
Bermuda	54	57,000
Cayman Islands	259	14,000
Cuba	114,524	9,995,000
Dominica	751	100,000
Dominican Republic	48,733	6,416,000
Grenada	344	113,000
Haiti	27,749	5,654,000
Jamaica	10,960	2,388,000
Montserrat	101	13,000
Netherlands Antilles	1,020	300,000
Puerto Rico	10,133	3,337,000
St Christopher Nevis	262	66,000
St Lucia	616	112,000
St Vincent	389	100,000
Trinidad and Tobago	5,128	1,167,000
Turks and Caicos Islands	430	6,000
Virgin Islands	392	105,000

Antigua

The flag was chosen when Antigua became an Associated State of the UK in 1967. The red stands for vigour, blue for hope, black for the people, yellow for the sun and beaches.

St Vincent

On full independence, this former Associated State of Great Britain chose a new vertical tricolour with its coat of arms on a breadfruit leaf on the central stripe.

Barbados

The truncated trident head comes from the pre-independence colonial badge. Adopted in 1966, the colours stand for the island's blue sea, blue sky and golden beaches.

Grenada

Adopted on independence in 1974, the flag illustrates the nutmeg, the main product. The stars stand for the seven parishes of the island. The colours stand for the sun, agriculture and the friendly people.

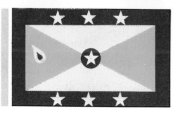

Netherlands Antilles

The six stars stand for the six islands of self-governing Netherlands Antilles. The colours, identical to the Dutch flag, show the close links that remain with the Netherlands. The flag was adopted in 1959.

Trinidad and Tobago

Adopted on independence in 1962, the red stands for the people's warmth and vitality, black for its strength and the islands' wealth, white for the sea and the people's hopes.

Flags of Africa

Egypt

Egypt joined with Syria and Libya in 1972 to form the Federation of Arab Republics and adopted a common flag of red, black and white – the colours of Arab nationalism. The emblem is Syrian.

Libya

The Libyan Arab Republic flew the flag of the Federation of Arab Republics until 1977 when it left the Federation. The plain green represents the nation's hope for a green revolution in agriculture.

Algeria

The flag, with its traditional Islamic symbol and colours, has flown since independence in 1962. It appeared in 1928 during the independence struggles, but the design may have been based on a far earlier patriotic flag.

Tunisia

The traditional symbols of the Muslim religion – the star and crescent – are in the centre of the flag which dates from the early 19th century. It was officially adopted on independence in 1956.

Morocco

The red flag was used for three centuries before the green Seal of Solomon was added in 1915. Morocco achieved independence in 1956.

AFRICA					
Algeria	2,766,889	21,351,000	Malawi	118,484	6,829,000
Angola	1,246,699	7,741,000	Mali	1,204,026	6,035,000
Benin	112,620	3,894,000	Mauritania	1,030,700	1,623,000
Botswana	600,372	1,033,000	Mauritius	2,046	1,009,000
Burundi	27,834	4,663,000	Morocco	446,549	23,565,000
Cameroon	475,441	9,507,000	Mozambique	801,589	13,402,000
Cape Verde	4,032	308,000	Niger	1,266,999	6,284,000
Central African Republic	622,983	2,892,000	Nigeria	923,773	63,000,000
Chad	1,284,000	5,116,000	Rwanda	26,337	6,017,000
Comoro Islands	2,145	456,000	St Helena	121	6,000
Congo	338,037	1,745,000	São Tomé and Principé	964	77,000
Djibouti	21,999	289,000	Senegal	196,192	6,541,000
Egypt	1,001,449	47,049,000	Seychelles	259	62,000
Equatorial Guinea	28,049	275,000	Sierra Leone	71,740	3,784,000
Ethiopia	1,221,899	31,998,000	Somalia	637,658	6,393,000
Gabon	267,666	792,000	South Africa	1,221,037	31,698,000
Gambia	11,294	725,000	Sudan	2,505,813	17,000,000
Ghana	238,536	13,804,000	Swaziland	17,363	651,000
Guinea	245,956	5,579,000	Tanzania	945,085	21,048,000
Guinea-Bissau	36,125	842,000	Togo	56,000	2,927,000
Ivory Coast	322,462	9,664,000	Tunisia	163,610	7,178,000
Kenya	582,646	19,372,000	Uganda	236,037	14,265,000
Lesotho	30,354	1,474,000	Upper Volta	274,123	7,100,000
Liberia	111,370	2,160,000	Zaire	2,671,410	32,054,000
Libya	1,759,537	2,400,000	Zambia	857,222	6,554,000
Malagasy Republic	587,044	8,000,000	Zimbabwe	444,868	8,383,000

Sudan

Based on the post 1918 Arab revolt flag, this design has been flown since 1969. Added to the Pan-Arab colours is an Islamic green triangle to symbolise material prosperity and spiritual wealth.

Ethiopia

The tricolour was first flown as three separate pennants, one above the other. The rectangular flag was used from 1897 with the red stripe at the top. The present order has been used since 1941.

Djibuti

Djibuti (formerly Afars and Issas) gained independence from France in 1977. Its flag has two horizontal stripes, a white triangle in the hoist, with a five-pointed red star. It has been in use since 1972 when it symbolised the wish for independence.

Somalia

British Somaliland (in the north) united with Somalia (in the south) in 1960 to form today's Somalia. The simple flag of the southern region of the country was adopted by the new country.

Kenya

Based on the flag of the Kenya African National Union which led the independence struggle, the design was adopted in 1963. The masai warrior's shield and two crossed spears stand for defence of freedom.

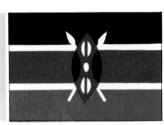

Uganda

The colours of the Uganda People's Congress were used for the national flag when the country gained independence in 1962. They represented the people (black), the sun (yellow), and brotherhood (red). A crested crane stands in the centre.

Tanzania

Tanganyika joined with Zanzibar to form Tanzania in 1964. The new flag has parts of the old flags of the two countries.

Rwanda

The tricolour of Pan-African colours adopted on independence in 1962 has an 'R' in the centre to distinguish it from the flag of Guinea.

Burundi

Introduced at the start of the Republic in 1966, the stars symbolise the nation's motto 'Unity, Work, Progress'. The colours represent peace (white), hope (green) and the struggle for independence (red).

Mauritania

Adopted in 1959 just before independence from France in 1960, the star and crescent reflect the Muslim religion followed by the majority. The country's official name is the Mauritanian Islamic Republic.

Mali

A French colony (French Sudan) until 1960, the Pan-African colours, used by the African Democratic Rally before independence, were arranged in the form of the French tricolour.

Senegal

Apart from the green five-pointed star which represents the people's Islamic faith, the flag is identical to Mali's. It was adopted in 1960 when the country gained its independence from France.

The Gambia

This former British colony, locked within Senegal, follows the course of the Gambia River. The flag, adopted in 1965, shows the blue river flowing through the green land with the sun overhead.

Guinea-Bissau

Adopted on independence from Portugal in 1973, the flag had been used since 1961 by the liberation movement. The colours are Pan-African.

Guinea

A former French colony, the design of the Republic's flag is based on the French tricolour, but using the Pan-African colours – red (for work), yellow (justice) and green (solidarity).

Sierra Leone

The colours of the flag that was adopted on independence from Britain in 1961 are derived from the coat of arms. Green stands for agriculture, white for peace and blue for the Atlantic Ocean which washes its shores.

Liberia

Founded in the early 19th century for freed black slaves from America, the flag adopted in 1847 was based on the Stars and Stripes, but has eleven stripes and a single white five-pointed star.

Ivory Coast

Like Guinea, Senegal, Mali and Cameroon, this former French colony adopted a flag based on the vertical stripes of the French tricolour on independence in 1959.

Upper Volta

The three main rivers of the country are the Black, White and Red Volta, and these colours were used for the flag adopted on independence in 1959.

Ghana

The colours, first hoisted by Ethiopia in 1894, were adopted by other former colonies as a sign of Pan-African unity after Ghana took the lead on independence in 1957.

Togo

The Togo Republic, which gained independence in 1960, flies the Pan-African colours – green stands for agriculture, yellow for mineral wealth and red for bloodshed. The white star stands for national purity.

Benin

In 1975 Benin became a People's Republic. The new flag is green with a red star in the upper hoist. The old Dahomey flag sported the red, yellow and green Pan-African colours.

Nigeria

The design was selected ahead of Nigeria's independence from Britain in 1960. The green stands for the country's forests and white is for peace.

Niger

Adopted in 1959 before independence from France in 1960, the orange disc in the centre represents the sun, the orange stripe the Sahara desert in the north, the white stands for goodness and purity, and the green for the grass of the south.

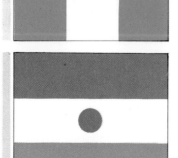

Cape Verde Islands

Formerly a Portuguese colony, the Pan-African flag was adopted in 1975. The emblem's five-pointed black star is above a garland of maize sheaves, two corn cobs and a clamshell.

Chad

Adopted in 1959, the colours are a compromise between those of France and Africa. Blue represents the sky, streams and hope, yellow the sun and desert, red the national sacrifice.

Cameroon

The Cameroons were formerly administered by Britain and France. When the French Cameroons became independent in 1960 the tricolour was adopted. Two stars were added when the British joined in 1961, to be replaced in 1975 by a single star.

Central African Republic

The flag was adopted when the country gained independence from France in 1960. It combines African and French colours to show the need for friendship.

Equatorial Guinea

Adopted in 1968, green is for the natural resources and wealth of the land, blue is for the sea, white is for peace and and red for the nation's struggle for independence.

São Tomé and Principe

These two islands gained independence from Portugal in 1975. The five-pointed stars in the tricolour stand for the two islands.

Gabon

Adopted on independence from France in 1960, the green stands for the country's forests and lumber industry, the blue for the sea, and the yellow for the sun.

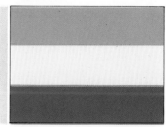

Congo

Independence was achieved in 1960 and ten years later the People's Republic was created, with a new red flag and emblem. The colours are the Pan-African colours – red, yellow and green. A hammer and hoe (rather than a sickle) represent industry and agriculture.

Zaire

The Pan-African colours were adopted by Zaire in 1971. The arm in the centre, originally the Popular Movement's emblem, holds a blazing torch – as a reminder of the spirit of revolution and the lives of dead revolutionaries.

St Helena

The emblem of this British Dependent Territory's flag has a trading ship, flying the flag of St George, between two huge volcanic rocks.

Angola

The flag is based on that of the Popular Movement for the Liberation of Angola during the country's struggle for independence which came in 1975. The half gear wheel and machete are reminiscent of the Soviet hammer and sickle.

Zambia

Adopted on independence in 1964, the eagle stands for freedom. The colours are those of the party that led the independence struggle.

Malawi

The colours of the flag were used by the Malawi Congress Party and when the country became independent in 1964 they were adopted for the national flag. The rising sun was added to indicate a new era.

Namibia

The country is under the control of South Africa and flies the South African national flag, although the United Nations are pressing for its independence – and for a flag of its own.

Design
Awaited

Botswana

When the country became independent in 1966, the markings of the zebra were chosen to express the equality of black and white people. Blue represents the nation's most vital need – rainwater.

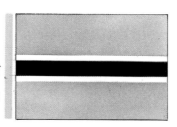

Zimbabwe

Adopted after legal independence in 1980, the new flag includes colours from the independence movements' flags and a white triangle for the minority population with the soapstone bird emblem.

Mozambique

The colours of FRELIMO were adopted in 1975. The rifle in the emblem stands for defence, the hoe for agriculture, the book for education, the cog wheel for industry.

South Africa

Since 1928 South Africa has flown a flag that has its origins with the first Dutch settlers. On the central stripe are the Union Flag, the flag of the old Orange Free State, and the flag of the Transvaal.

Lesotho

Adopted in 1966 on independence from Britain, the blue stands for rain, the red for faith in the future, the green for the land. The central emblem is a traditional conical woven straw hat.

Swaziland

Flown since independence in 1968, the flag is based on that of the Swazi Pioneer Corps. The emblem has the weapons of a warrior – the ox-hide shield, two assegai (throwing spears) and a fighting stick.

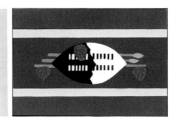

Comoros

The flag flown since independence from France in 1975 reflects the islanders' Muslim faith. The stars represent the four islands, although Mayotte remains a French Dependency.

Seychelles

A new flag was adopted in 1977. The wavy design is said to suggest the Indian Ocean in which the Seychelles Islands lie.

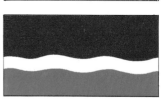

Malagasy Republic

Madagascar's people came from South-East Asia and brought the historic red and white colours with them. The present flag was adopted in 1958 when the Malagasy Republic was formed on the island of Madagascar.

Mauritius

The flag was adopted on independence in 1968. Red is for the people's struggle and bloodshed, blue for the Indian Ocean, yellow for the bright future and green for the vegetation.

Flags of Oceania

Fiji
Independent since 1970, Fiji retains the British Ensign. Its own coat of arms shows a British lion, sugar cane, a coconut palm, bananas and a dove of peace.

Vanuatu
On independence from both Britain and France in 1980, Vanuatu (formerly New Hebrides) adopted an original design which has a boar's horn in the triangle in the hoist.

Tonga
The flag was adopted in 1875 on the understanding that it would never be changed. Symbolising the islanders' Christianity, it was retained on independence.

Nauru
The flag shows this tiny island's position just south of the Equator. The 12 points of the star represent the 12 tribes of Nauru.

Kiribati
Since 1979 the flag has consisted solely of the coat of arms. It shows a frigate bird flying over the sun as it rises over the Pacific Ocean.

Tuvalu
Formerly the Ellice Islands, Tuvalu's flag retains the Union flag and shows the position of the nine main islands in the group.

Solomon Islands
Adopted on independence in 1978, the flag has a star for each island on a blue (sea) and green (land) field, with a yellow (sun) stripe.

Western Samoa
The flag returns to the red and white of the pre-colonial flags of the kingdom of Samoa. The stars represent the Southern Cross constellation.

Australia
The national flag has the Union flag showing the link with Great Britain, the stars of the Southern Cross constellation and the seven-pointed Commonwealth Star – one point for each of the original States and one for the Dependent Territories. The predominately blue and white flag also echoes the banner of the Eureka Stockade gold miners against government corruption and oppression in the nineteenth century.

The States have the Blue Ensign with their own badges:

New South Wales – St George's Cross with a lion and four eight-pointed stars;

Queensland – blue Maltese Cross with royal crown;

South Australia – white-backed piping shrike (the Murray magpie);

Tasmania – red lion;

Victoria – a crown over the Southern Cross;

Western Australia – black swan on a yellow field;

Northern Territory – created in 1978, it has a distinctive flag with the Southern Cross and a desert rose on a brownish background.

OCEANIA					
American Samoa	197	31,000	New Zealand	268,746	3,251,000
Australia	7,686,845	15,462,000	Niue	259	4,000
Cook Islands	241	18,000	Northern Marianas	479	14,000
Federated States of Micronesia	1,800	102,000	Papua New Guinea	461,690	3,226,000
Fiji	18,272	686,000	Solomon Islands	29,785	263,000
Guam	616	115,000	Tonga	699	105,000
Kiribati	956	58,000	Tuvalu	25	8,000
Nauru	21	8,000	Vanuatu	14,763	130,000
			Western Samoa	2,841	162,000

New Zealand
The flag was designed in 1869 and retained on independence in 1917. Based on the British Blue Ensign, it has four of the five stars of the Southern Cross.

Cook Islands
The flag has a circle of 15 stars – one for each island in the group – and was adopted in 1973 eight years after independence from New Zealand.

Niue
A self-governing dependency of New Zealand, Niue's bright yellow flag indicates warmth towards New Zealand and the Commonwealth.

Federated States of Micronesia
Formerly the Trust Territory of the Pacific Islands, these islands are administered by the United States. The four stars stand for the four territories.

Northern Marianas
A Commonwealth of the United States, its flag shows a white star in front of a *taga*, a chalice-shaped stone symbol of its ancient Polynesian inhabitants.

American Samoa
The islands are an American dependency and were granted their own government in 1960. The bald eagle holds a Samoan chief's staff and knife.

Guam
This island and base has been a dependency of the United States since 1898. The flag with its desert island picture is flown only with the US flag.

Papua New Guinea
The red and black flag is halved diagonally. A bird of paradise in flight is depicted in gold on the red and the stars of the Southern Cross constellation in white on the black.

Flags of Europe

Switzerland
A square red flag with a white Greek Cross is the national flag of Switzerland, dating back to 1848. But the cross as the emblem of the Swiss is much older than this. In the 14th century, Swiss soldiers wore 'the sign of the Holy Cross, a white cross on a red shield'. The flag of the International Red Cross is based on the Swiss flag.

France
The colours of the French flag originated in the cockades worn during the revolution. They were adopted in 1789 and a flag incorporating them appeared in 1790. It was white, with a red, white and blue canton. In 1794 a call for a simpler flag, appropriate to republican morals, ideas and principles, resulted in the present tricolour.

Monaco
The colours of the flag come from the Prince of Monaco's coat of arms. Monaco has been an independent state since 980 AD but the present flag was adopted in 1881.

Belgium
The colours date from the arms of the Province of Brabant (a gold lion with red tongue on a black shield). Today's almost square flag was adopted in 1830 on independence from the Dutch.

Netherlands
Before 1630, the followers of William of Orange flew an orange, white and blue flag. Red replaced the orange and the Dutch tricolour became a symbol of liberty.

Luxembourg
The flag of the Grand Duchy has similar colours to that of the Netherlands, but the flag is longer and the blue lighter. The colours were taken from the Grand Duke's 13th century coat of arms.

Ireland
First used by nationalists in the 1800's, green stands for the Catholics, orange for the Protestants and white for the much hoped for peace between them.

Liechtenstein

The colours date back to the early 19th century. The gold crown was added in 1937 to avoid confusion with the flag flown by Haiti at that time.

Germany, West

The colours, dating back to the Holy Roman Empire and associated with the struggle for a united Germany from the 1830's, were re-adopted in 1949.

Austria

The flag was adopted in 1918 but the colours may date from the Battle of Ptolemais in 1191. It is said that the only part of the Duke of Bebenberg's white tunic not stained with blood was that under his sword belt.

United Kingdom

The Union flag combines English, Scottish and Irish emblems – but not one for Wales. The first Union flag dates from 1603, when James VI of Scotland became James I of England. The St. George's cross of England (1) and the St Andrew's cross of Scotland (3) formed the first Union flag. When Ireland was united with Great Britain in 1801, an Irish emblem was added to form the Union flag as we know it today. The red cross of St George has been used in England since the 13th century and St Andrew's flag of Scotland is probably even older. The white star in the centre of the flag of Northern Ireland (2) has six points representing the counties of Northern Ireland. The red dragon of Cadwallader, Prince of Gwynnedd, on a field of white and green, was officially recognised as the Welsh flag in 1959 (4).

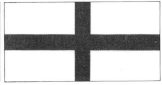
1

2

3

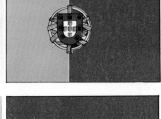
4

Italy

When Napoleon invaded Italy in 1796, the French Guard had a standard of vertical green, white and red. The flag was finally established as that of a united Italy in 1861.

Vatican City

Headquarters of the Roman Catholic Church, the flag bears the triple tiara of the Popes above the keys of Heaven given to St Peter.

San Marino

The Republic has been an independent State since AD 885. The white is for the snowy mountains, the blue for the sky.

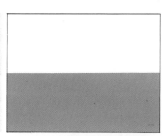

Portugal

The colours adopted in the revolution in 1910 represent Henry the Navigator (green) and the monarchy (red). The armillary shield – a navigational instrument – indicates Portugal's lead in exploration.

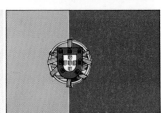

Spain

The present design, with the yellow stripe twice the width of the red stripes, was adopted in 1938, but the colours date back to the old kingdom of Aragon in the 12th century.

Malta

The colours are from the arms of the Knights of St John. The George Cross was added in 1943, to commemorate the heroism of the Maltese in World War II. The present design dates from independence in 1964.

Gibraltar

Gibraltar, a UK dependency since 1713, flies the Union Flag officially, but the city flag symbolizing the fortified gateway to the Mediterranean is more often seen.

Greece

Since 1975 the national flag has been a white cross on a blue background. The striped flag – used from 1970 to 1975 – is now the civil and naval ensign.

Cyprus

Designed to avoid disunity between the Greek and Turkish communities on independence in 1960, the island is drawn over two olive branches. The separate communities fly the Greek and Turkish flags today.

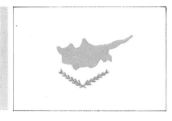

Finland

The design was adopted when Finland gained independence from Russia in 1917. The Scandinavian blue cross is slightly off-centre towards the hoist.

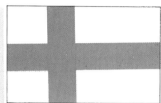

Sweden

The flag of Sweden has been flown since the reign of King Gustavus in the 16th century, but was not officially adopted until 1906. The colours come from the state coat of arms dating back to 1364.

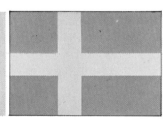

Norway

First adopted in 1821, the flag was not generally used until 1898. It is based on the flag of Denmark, to which Norway once belonged.

Denmark

Legend has it that King Waldemar II saw a white cross against a red sky in battle in 1219. His forces went on to win and the Dannebrog ('the spirit of Denmark') has been used continuously since.

Faroes

Adopted in 1948, the cross is like that on other Scandinavian flags – slightly off-centre. The Faroes remain part of the Danish realm.

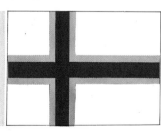

Iceland

Traditionally Iceland's colours are blue and white. The present colours are a combination of those of Denmark, Norway and the coat of arms. Dating from 1915, it became the official flag on independence in 1944.

Soviet Union

The plain red flag has the hammer (industry) and sickle (agriculture) and the star (Communist Party). The flag is unchanged since 1923.

Poland

The red and white of Poland's flag come from the 13th century national emblem – a white eagle on a red field. The flag was adopted when Poland became a republic in 1919.

East Germany

In 1959 the state emblem of the German Democratic Republic was added to the old German flag (of 1949).

Czechoslovakia

The flag combines the red and white of Bohemia with blue – one of the colours of Moravia and Slovakia. First used in a horizontal tricolour by Slovakia in 1848, today's design dates from 1920.

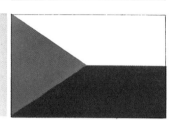

Hungary

The plain tricolour was first adopted in 1948, though it was widely used before then. The colours date from the 9th century.

EUROPE		
Albania	28,749	2,906,000
Austria	83,848	7,544,000
Belgium	30,512	9,872,000
Bulgaria	110,911	8,969,000
Cyprus	9,251	661,000
Czechoslovakia	127,868	15,466,000
Denmark	43,069	5,112,000
Faroe Islands	1,399	41,000
Finland	337,008	4,873,000
France	547,026	54,872,000
German Democratic Republic	108,179	16,718,000
German Federal Republic	248,577	61,387,000
Gibraltar	6	30,000
Greece	131,944	9,984,000
Hungary	93,030	10,681,000
Iceland	102,999	239,000
Ireland, Republic of	69,000	3,440,000
Italy	301,224	56,998,000
Liechtenstein	161	24,000
Luxembourg	2,585	366,000
Malta	315	356,000
Monaco	1.46	25,000
Netherlands	40,844	14,437,000
Norway	324,218	4,145,000
Poland	312,677	36,887,000
Portugal	92,082	10,045,000
Romania	237,500	22,683,000
San Marino	60	20,000
Soviet Union	22,402,194	275,093,000
Spain	504,780	38,435,000
Sweden	449,963	8,335,000
Switzerland	41,287	6,477,000
United Kingdom	244,045	56,023,000
Vatican City	0.44	1,000
Yugoslavia	267,141	22,997,000

Yugoslavia

In 1918 several states formed the new kingdom of Yugoslavia. The colours come from the flags of these states. In 1946 the coat of arms was replaced by the Communist star.

Romania

The colours come from the arms of the provinces that united to form Romania in 1861. The coat of arms shows the country's natural resources – forests, oil, wheat, mountains.

Bulgaria

A tricolour of white, green and red dates from 1878 – colours used in Slav countries at that time. The national emblem was first added to the flag in 1947. The lion has been a symbol of Bulgaria since the 14th century.

Albania

The name Albania means 'land of the eagle'. The flag bears a two-headed black eagle emblem on a dark red ground. The Communist star above the eagle was added in 1945.

Flags of Asia

Indonesia

The red and white colours go back to the Middle Ages, a symbol of revolution then and of the struggle for independence in modern times. Indonesia became independent of the Netherlands in 1945.

Singapore

The flag dates from 1959 when self-government was introduced. The crescent stands for the young country's ascent and the stars for its aspirations to democracy, peace, progress, justice and equality.

Malaysia

The 14 stripes and points of the star stand for the 13 states and capital territory of Kuala Lumpur. The crescent and star are symbols of Islam.

Brunei

When the British took over in 1906 a white and a black stripe were added to the Sultan's plain yellow flag. In 1959 the state arms were added.

Philippines

The eight rays of the sun stand for the eight provinces that revolted against Spanish rule in 1898. The stars represent the three main island groups.

Thailand

Two red and white stripes are all that remain of Thailand's traditional red on white elephant emblem. The blue stripe, added in 1917, showed solidarity with the Allies, whose flags had the same colours.

Vietnam

A yellow star on a red field was the flag of Ho Chi-minh in World War II. In 1945 it became the national flag. Today, with a slight variation made to the star in 1955, it still flies over Vietnam – north and south.

Kampuchea

Though in keeping with the Communist regime, the red flag is traditional. So too is the emblem of the Great Temple of Angkor Wat which appears in gold.

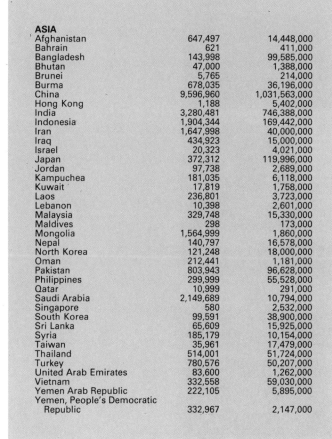

ASIA		
Afghanistan	647,497	14,448,000
Bahrain	621	411,000
Bangladesh	143,998	99,585,000
Bhutan	47,000	1,388,000
Brunei	5,765	214,000
Burma	678,035	36,196,000
China	9,596,960	1,031,563,000
Hong Kong	1,188	5,402,000
India	3,280,481	746,388,000
Indonesia	1,904,344	169,442,000
Iran	1,647,998	40,000,000
Iraq	434,923	15,000,000
Israel	20,323	4,021,000
Japan	372,312	119,996,000
Jordan	97,738	2,689,000
Kampuchea	181,035	6,118,000
Kuwait	17,819	1,758,000
Laos	236,801	3,723,000
Lebanon	10,398	2,601,000
Malaysia	329,748	15,330,000
Maldives	298	173,000
Mongolia	1,564,999	1,860,000
Nepal	140,797	16,578,000
North Korea	121,248	18,000,000
Oman	212,441	1,181,000
Pakistan	803,943	96,628,000
Philippines	299,999	55,528,000
Qatar	10,999	291,000
Saudi Arabia	2,149,689	10,794,000
Singapore	580	2,532,000
South Korea	99,591	38,900,000
Sri Lanka	65,609	15,925,000
Syria	185,179	10,154,000
Taiwan	35,961	17,479,000
Thailand	514,001	51,724,000
Turkey	780,576	50,207,000
United Arab Emirates	83,600	1,262,000
Vietnam	332,558	59,030,000
Yemen Arab Republic	222,105	5,895,000
Yemen, People's Democratic Republic	332,967	2,147,000

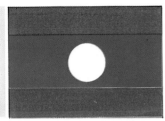

Laos
The flag of the Pathet Lao was adopted in 1979 when Laos became a Communist republic. The blue stands for the Mekong River, the white disc for the moon and the red for the unity and purpose of the people.

Burma
In 1974 a new socialist symbol appeared on the flag. A ring of 14 stars representing the 14 states surrounds a gearwheel and a rice plant, representing industry and agriculture.

Bhutan
The name Bhutan means 'Land of the Dragon', hence the strange creature in the middle of the flag. The saffron yellow colour represents royal power, and the orange-red represents Buddhist spiritual power.

Taiwan
Originally Sun Yat-sen's flag, the nationalists fought under the 'white sun in blue sky over red land' against the Communists. When they were forced to retreat to Taiwan, they took the flag with them.

China
Red – the traditional colour of China and of Communism – was chosen for the People's flag in 1949. The big star stands for the party's Common Programme, the small ones for the four social classes it unites.

Hong Kong
The British Blue Ensign has flown over Hong Kong since 1841. The coat of arms, dating from 1959, includes British lion and Chinese dragon.

Mongolia
Communist red appears with blue, the Mongolian national colour. The gold star of the Communist Party tops the *soyonbo*, the traditional symbol of Mongolia.

North Korea
The Korean Democratic People's Republic was founded in 1948. The colours are those of the original flag, but in a new Communist pattern with a star.

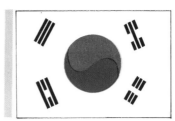

South Korea
Adopted in 1950, the flag is the traditional white of peace. The central symbol stands for nature's opposing forces. The black symbols stand for the four seasons, the points of the compass and the sun, moon, earth and heaven.

Japan
The Land of the Rising Sun's flag was officially adopted in 1870 but it had been used by emperors in Japan for centuries before.

Nepal
This Himalayan kingdom has the only national flag that is not rectangular in shape. Two separate pennants were joined in the 19th century and the present design – retaining the crescent moon and sun – was adopted in 1962.

Afghanistan
After many recent changes, Afghanistan has reverted to its traditional colours with the state arms in the canton.

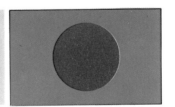

Bangladesh
Following the break with Pakistan in 1971, the new flag has a green field (for fertile land) and a red disc that represents the struggle for freedom.

Pakistan
Green is the traditional colour of Islam. The flag, adopted on independence in 1947, is green with the Muslim crescent and star. But a white stripe is left to represent the other religions and minorities.

India
Originally the Indian National Congress Flag, the orange represents the Hindu majority, green the Muslims, white the wish for peace between them. The Buddhist wheel symbol was added on independence in 1947.

Sri Lanka
The flag of this Buddhist nation includes the lion banner of the ancient kingdom, and two stripes for the island's minority groups, green for the Muslims, orange for the Hindus.

Maldives
A Muslim country, the island's flag was originally plain red. Early this century an Islamic green panel with white crescent was added. The present design was adopted in 1965.

Turkey
The crescent has appeared on flags of Turkey for centuries, but the star was added only in the mid 1800's. The flag was kept when the Ottoman Empire became the republic of Turkey in 1923.

Syria
Syria with Egypt jointly made up the Federation of Arab Republics. Both countries fly the same flag which has been used since 1972 but Syria's new link with Libya probably means a change of flag.

Lebanon
The cedar tree has been a symbol of Lebanon since the days of the Bible. The tree was included in the flag when the country became independent in 1943. The colours are those of the Lebanese Legion.

Israel
The blue and white stripes are from the Hebrew prayer-shawl and the Star of David is in the centre. Designed in the late 1800's in the United States it was adopted by the new state in 1948.

Jordan
Based on the flag of the Arab revolt, the present design was adopted in 1921. The points of the star stand for the first verses of the Koran.

Iraq
Designed in 1963 with the Pan-Arab colours, the idea was that Iraq, with Syria and Egypt, would have the same flag. The three stars stand for the three countries, but their unity is still awaited.

Iran
The tricolour was adopted in the early years of this century. The lion and sun symbol does not appear on the flag even though it is the most revered Iranian emblem.

Saudi Arabia
The design was adopted in 1938. Above the white sword, the inscription reads: 'There is no god but Allah, and Muhammad is the Prophet of Allah'. The flag is double so that it can be read from both sides.

Bahrain
In 1820 the British requested friendly states around the Persian Gulf to have white on their flags. This is separated from the traditional Muslim red by a serrated line.

Qatar
Used since the mid-19th century, the maroon colour results from the natural effect of the sun on the traditional red.

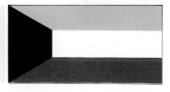

Kuwait
Independence was achieved in 1961, when Kuwait ceased to be a British Protectorate. The new flag has the four Pan-Arab colours.

United Arab Emirates
The Pan-Arab colours were a natural choice for the seven small states of the Persian Gulf which formed the United Arab Emirates in 1971.

Oman
Formerly Muscat and Oman, the state's flag was a traditional red. In 1970, when the State of Oman was established, the State arms of swords and a dagger were added with stripes of white and green.

People's Democratic Republic of Yemen
The National Liberation Front's flag was red, white and black. When they forced the British to leave Aden in 1967, they added the pale blue triangle and red star.

Yemen Arab Republic
Like the people's republic, the flag is based on the Arab revolt flag (see Egypt). In 1962 the flag, with one green star, was adopted with Arab unity in mind.

MAPS

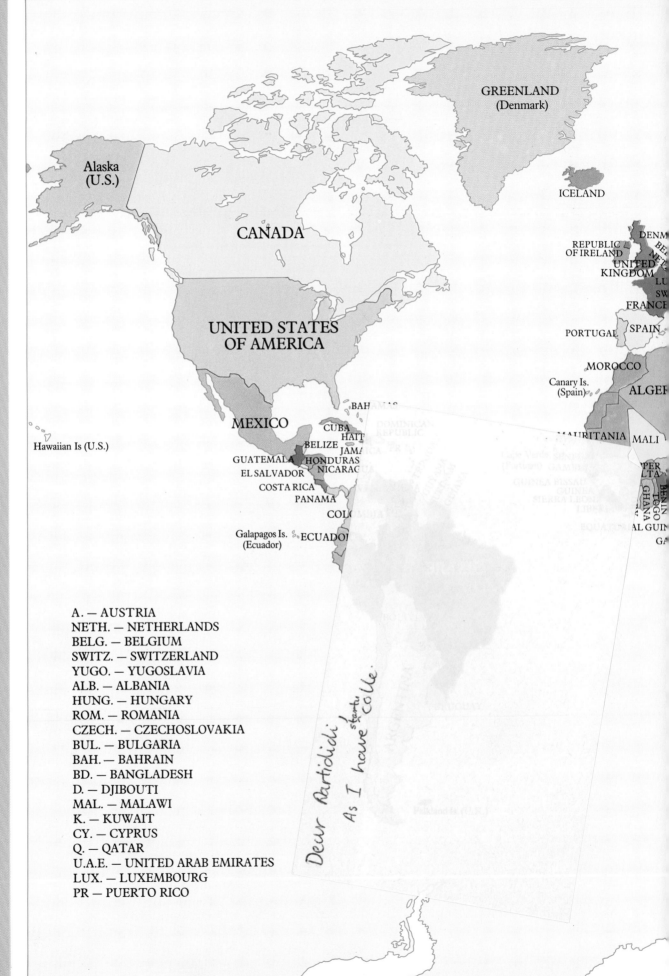

GREENLAND
(Denmark)

Alaska
(U.S.)

ICELAND

CANADA

DENM
REPUBLIC
OF IRELAND
UNITED
KINGDOM
FRANCE

PORTUGAL SPAIN

MOROCCO
Canary Is.
(Spain) ALGER

UNITED STATES
OF AMERICA

MAURITANIA MALI

BAH
CUBA
HAIT
MEXICO BELIZE JAMA
Hawaiian Is (U.S.) GUATEMALA HONDURAS
EL SALVADOR NICARAG
COSTA RICA
PANAMA
COL

Galapagos Is. ECUADOR
(Ecuador)

A. — AUSTRIA
NETH. — NETHERLANDS
BELG. — BELGIUM
SWITZ. — SWITZERLAND
YUGO. — YUGOSLAVIA
ALB. — ALBANIA
HUNG. — HUNGARY
ROM. — ROMANIA
CZECH. — CZECHOSLOVAKIA
BUL. — BULGARIA
BAH. — BAHRAIN
BD. — BANGLADESH
D. — DJIBOUTI
MAL. — MALAWI
K. — KUWAIT
CY. — CYPRUS
Q. — QATAR
U.A.E. — UNITED ARAB EMIRATES
LUX. — LUXEMBOURG
PR — PUERTO RICO

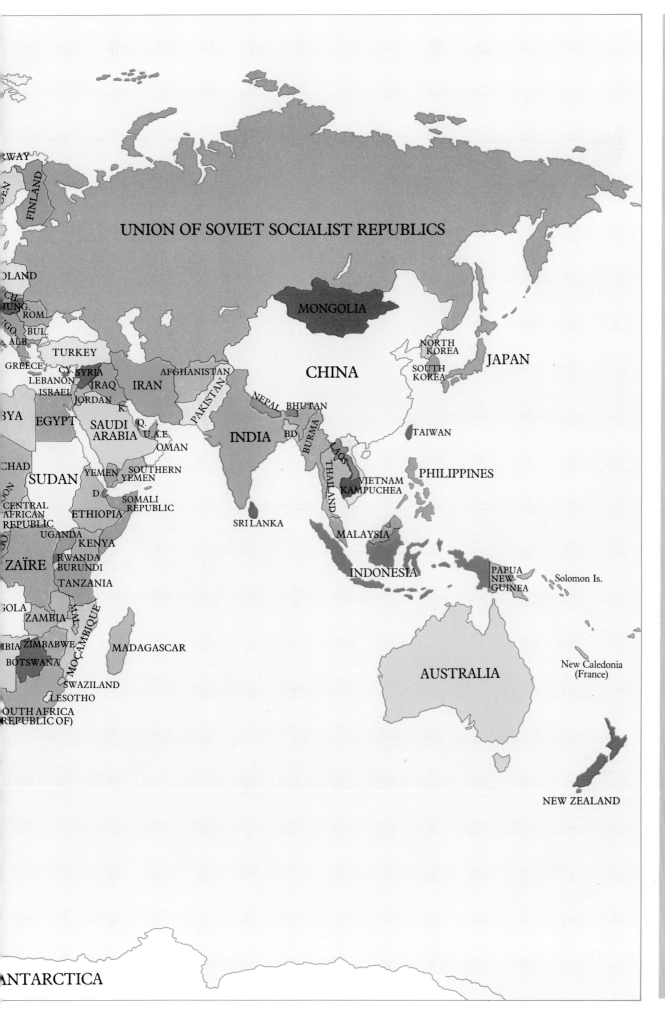

RWAY

EN

FINLAND

OLAND

CH.

UNG.

GO. BUL.

ALB.

GREECE

LEBANON

ISRAEL

BYA

EGYPT

CHAD

SUDAN

CENTRAL
AFRICAN
REPUBLIC

ZAÏRE

GOLA

ZAMBIA

IBIA

BOTSWANA

SOUTH AFRICA
(REPUBLIC OF)

TURKEY

CY. SYRIA

IRAQ

JORDAN

K.

SAUDI
ARABIA

Q.

U.A.E.

OMAN

YEMEN

D.

SOMALI
REPUBLIC

ETHIOPIA

UGANDA

KENYA

RWANDA
BURUNDI

TANZANIA

MW

MOÇAMBIQUE

ZIMBABWE

SWAZILAND

LESOTHO

SOUTHERN
YEMEN

MADAGASCAR

UNION OF SOVIET SOCIALIST REPUBLICS

MONGOLIA

CHINA

NORTH
KOREA

SOUTH
KOREA

JAPAN

AFGHANISTAN

IRAN

PAKISTAN

NEPAL

BHUTAN

INDIA

BD

BURMA

TAIWAN

LAOS

THAILAND

VIETNAM

KAMPUCHEA

PHILIPPINES

SRI LANKA

MALAYSIA

INDONESIA

PAPUA
NEW
GUINEA

Solomon Is.

AUSTRALIA

New Caledonia
(France)

NEW ZEALAND

ANTARCTICA

65°

A | B | C | D | ARCTIC | E

30°

ICELAND

Arctic Circle

NORWEGIAN SEA

S C A N D I N A V I

55°

▲ Galdhöpiggen
2469

NORWAY

Lake
Vänern

ATLANTIC

▲ Ben Nevis
1343

N O R T H

SWEDEN

20°

OCEAN

IRELAND

**UNITED
KINGDOM**

S E A

DENMARK

B A L T I C

S E A

NETHERLANDS

POLAN

Thames

**WEST
GERMANY**

EAST

N o r t h

Vistu

English Channel

BELGIUM

Rhine

Elbe

Oder

Seine

LUXEMBOURG

45°

Danube

CZECHOSLOVAKI

*Bay of
Biscay*

FRANCE

LIECHTENSTEIN

SWITZERLAND

AUSTRIA

Hunga

MASSIF

A L P S

HUNGA

Garonne

CENTRAL

Rhône

▲Mt Blanc
4807

Po

CANTABRIAN
MTS

MONACO

ITALY

SAN MARINO

Sava

Duero

PYRÉNÉES

ANDORRA

**LIGURIAN
SEA**

DINARIC ALPS

PORTUGAL

▲
Pico de Aneto
3404

Ebro

YUGOSLA

Tagus

SPAIN

*M
e
s
e
t
a*

A P E N N I N E S

ADRIATIC

ALBAN

Guadiana

SEA

Guadalquivir

SIERRA
NEVADA

TYRRHENIAN
SEA

35°

Str. of Gibraltar

M E D I T E R R A N E A N

IONIAN

▲Mt Etna
3340

SEA

TELL ATLAS

SEA

MOROCCO

ALGERIA

TUNISIA

MALTA

10°

0°

10°

F J G OCEAN H J J 1 K

Pechora

Narodynaya
1894

Ob

2

U R A L   M T S

West
Siberian
Plain

White Sea

70°

N. Dvina

Lake
Onega

FINLAND

Kama

Lake
Ladoga

Gulf of Finland

Volga

Ural

3

60°

Kirghiz
Steppe

U S S R

Central Russian Uplands

W. Dvina

ropean   Plain

Don

Dnieper

Donets

Volga

Dnestr

Ust Urt
Plateau

RPATHIANS

Sea of Azov

C A S P I A N   S E A

ain

ROMANIA

Elbrus
5633m

4

BULGARIA

B L A C K   S E A

CAUCASUS   MTS

ALKAN MTS

PONTINE   RANGE

Kizil

Mt Ararat
5165

mpus
911

TURKEY

ELBURZ MTS

AEGEAN
SEA

TAURUS MTS

Euphrates

Tigris

IRAN

GREECE

CYPRUS

SYRIA

IRAQ

5

50°

30°

40°

1

2

3

4

I

H

G

F

E

D

C

B

A

55°

54°

53°

NORTH SEA

IRISH SEA

North Channel

SOUTHERN UPLANDS

SCOTLAND

CHEVIOT HILLS

Hadrian's Wall

THE PENNINES

NORTH YORK MOORS

LAKE DISTRICT

THE FENS

THE BROADS

The Wash

Tweed

Tyne

Tees

Ouse

Trent

Trent

Witham

Severn

Dee

Solway Firth

Scafell Pike 978m

Snaefell 620m

Snowdon 1085m

Isle of Man

Anglesey

Holy Isle

MTS

Great Yarmouth
Cromer
Norwich
Sandringham
King's Lynn
Spalding
Peterborough
Grantham
Boston
Skegness
Cleethorpes
Grimsby
Spurn Head
Scunthorpe
Gainsborough
Lincoln
Newark-on-Trent
Loughborough
Leicester
Tamworth
Nottingham
Mansfield
Chesterfield
Burton upon Trent
Derby
Stafford
Telford
Shrewsbury
Walsall
Wolverhampton
Newcastle-under-Lyme
Stoke-on-Trent
Crewe
Chester
Connah's Quay
Denbigh
Wrexham
Ffestiniog
Bangor
Caernarfon
Llandudno Colwyn Bay
Holyhead
Pwllheli

Flamborough Head
Bridlington
Scarborough
Whitby
Kingston upon Hull
Goole
Doncaster
Barnsley
Rotherham
Sheffield
Wakefield
Huddersfield
Halifax
Bradford
Leeds
Harrogate
Ripon
York
Keighley
Burnley
Rochdale
Oldham
Manchester
Stockport
Buxton
Bolton
Blackburn
Wigan
Warrington
Runcorn
St. Helens
Liverpool
Wallasey
Birkenhead
Southport
Blackpool
Preston
Lancaster
Morecambe
Kendal
Barrow-in-Furness
Whitehaven
Workington
Keswick
Penrith
Carlisle

Middlesbrough and Teesside
Hartlepool
Stockton-on-Tees
Darlington
Durham
Sunderland
South Shields
Gateshead
Newcastle upon Tyne
Blyth
Ashington
Berwick-upon-Tweed

Galashiels
Hawick
Moffat
Dumfries
Motherwell
Kilmarnock
Prestwick
Ayr
Girvan
Stranraer
Campbeltown

Douglas

Ballycastle
Ballymena
Antrim
Larne
Belfast
Lisburn
Lurgan
Newry
Lough Neagh
Drogheda
Dublin
Dun Laoghaire
Wicklow

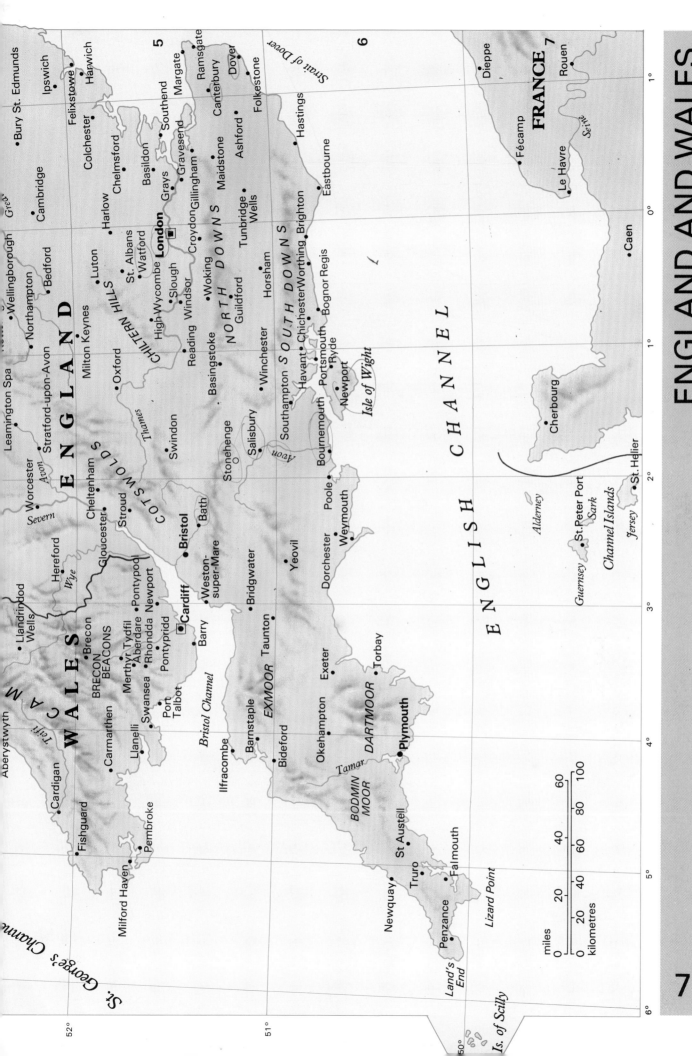

ENGLAND AND WALES

7

SCOTLAND

	A	B	C	D	E	F	G

Shetland Islands

Shetland Islands

Lerwick

at same scale 1°

miles
0   20   40   60
0   20   40   60   80   100
kilometres

ATLANTIC OCEAN

59°

60°

Orkney Islands

Kirkwall

Pentland Firth

John O'Groats

Thurso

Wick

NORTH SEA

Fair Isle

OUTER HEBRIDES

Stornoway

Lewis

Tarbert

Harris

58°

Ullapool

Loch Shin

Lairg

Helmsdale

Moray Firth

Cromarty

Dingwall

Nairn

Elgin

Banff

Fraserburgh

Keith

Peterhead

North Uist

Portree

Stromeferry

Inverness

NORTH WEST HIGHLANDS

Grantown-on-Spey

Huntly

Skye

Kyle of Lochalsh

Broadford

Loch Ness

Spey

Don

Aberdeen

South Uist

Dee

57°

Eriskay

Rhum

GLENMORE

CAIRNGORMS

Ben Macdhui 1311m

Ballater

Barra

Eigg

Fort William

Braemar

Stonehaven

INNER HEBRIDES

Coll

▲ Ben Nevis 1343m

GRAMPIAN MOUNTAINS

Pitlochry

Brechin

Montrose

Forfar

Tiree

Mull

Oban

Loch Tay

Tay

Dundee

Arbroath

Firth of Lorn

SCOTLAND

Perth

Firth of Tay

St. Andrews

Jura

Callander

Loch Lomond

Stirling

Glenrothes

56°

Kirkcaldy

Firth of Forth

Dunbar

Dumbarton

Dunfermline

Falkirk

Cumbernauld

Islay

Greenock

Clydebank

Glasgow

□ **Edinburgh**

Paisley

Coatbridge

Arran

Hamilton

Motherwell

Berwick-upon-Tweed

East Kilbride

Wishaw

Peebles

Galashiels

Firth of Clyde

Irvine

Kilmarnock

Clyde

Tweed

Ayr

Prestwick

SOUTHERN UPLANDS

North Channel

Campbeltown

Moffat

Hawick

Portrush

Girvan

Coleraine

NORTHERN IRELAND

55°

Dumfries

ENGLAND

Londonderry

Newton Stewart

Ballymena

Larne

Stranraer

Solway Firth

Carlisle

| 1 |
| 2 |
| 3 |
| 4 |
| 5 |
| 6 |

7°   6°   5°   4°   3°   2°

8

IRELAND

miles
0   20   40   60
0 20 40 60 80 100
kilometres

A   B   C   D   E   F

1

NORTHERN IRELAND

North Channel

Portrush
Ballycastle
Buncrana
Coleraine
Lough Foyle
Londonderry
Bann
Larne
Strabane
Ballymena
Antrim
Newtownabbey   Bangor
Belfast Lough
Donegal   Omagh   ☐ **Belfast**
Ballyshannon   Lough Neagh   Lisburn
Donegal Bay   Lower Lough Erne   Portadown • Lurgan
Enniskillen   Armagh
Sligo   Upper Lough Erne   Monaghan   Newry   Downpatrick

5°

2

Carrickmacross   Dundalk

IRISH

Ballina   Lough Conn
Carrick-on-Shannon

Achill Isle
Castlebar   Longford   Kells
Westport   Drogheda
Lough Mask   Roscommon •   **SEA**

4°

REPUBLIC OF IRELAND

3

Clifden   Lough Corrib   Lough Ree
Athlone   **Dublin** • Howth
Athenry   Clara   Liffey
Galway   Ballinasloe   Naas   Dun Laoghaire
Galway Bay   Kildare
Shannon   Port Laoise

3°

Aran Is   Lough Derg   Roscrea   Athy   Wicklow
Ennis   Nenagh   Carlow   Arklow
Kilkee   Thurles
Kilrush   Kilkenny
Limerick   Cashel   New Ross

WICKLOW MTS

4

Tipperary
Clonmel   Wexford
Tralee   Waterford

St. George's Channel

Blackwater
Dingle   Killarney   Mallow   Dungarvan
Dingle Bay   Youghal

2°

▲ Carrantuohill 1041m   Cork
Kenmare   Cobh
Bandon

Bantry Bay   Bantry

5

10°   9°   8°   7°   6°

9

A B C D E

ENGLAND

Dove

Southampton
Exeter
Portsmouth
Brighton
Bournemouth

Plymouth
Torbay
Isle of Wight

Penzance
Truro

50°

English Channel

Dieppe

Alderney

Cherbourg
Le Havre
Rou

Guernsey
Sark

Channel Islands
Br.
Jersey

St. Helier
Caen

Île d'Ouessant

Brest
Morlaix
St. Malo
Alençon

St. Brieuc

48°

Fougères

Quimper
Rennes

Le Mans

Lorient

F   FR

Vannes

Angers
Tours

Belle Île

St. Nazaire
Loire

Nantes
Cholet

Île de Noirmoutier

Châtellerault

Île d'Yeu

La Roche-
sur-Yon
Poitiers

46°

Île de Ré

Île d'Oléron

Cognac
Limoge

Angoulême

B a y   o f

Périgueu

B i s c a y

Gironde

miles
0   50   100

Bergerac
Bordeaux
Dordogne

0   50   100   150
kilometres

Lot

44°

Agen

Montaub

Gulf of Gascony

Dax
Adour

Toulou

Gijón
Santander
Biarritz
Bayonne

Oviedo
Torrelavega
San Sebastián
Pau
Tarbes

Bilbao
Lourdes

S P A I N
Vitoria

P Y R É N É E S

Pamplona
*Pic de
Vignemale*
3298 ▲

Pico de Aneto
3404 ▲

G

6°   4°   2°   0°

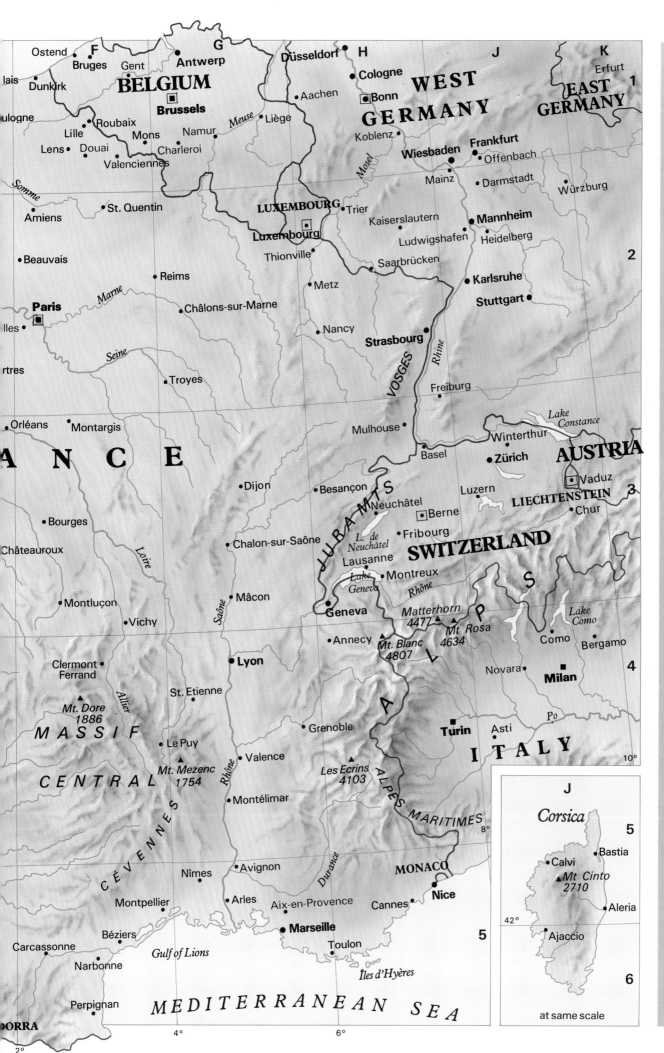

BELGIUM
Ostend
Bruges
Gent
Antwerp
F
G
Düsseldorf
H
Cologne
J
WEST
Erfurt
K
EAST
GERMANY
1
Aachen
Bonn
GERMANY
Dunkirk
lais
Boulogne
Roubaix
Lille
Mons
Lens Douai
Valenciennes
Brussels
Namur
Charleroi
Liège
Meuse
Koblenz
Mosel
Wiesbaden
Frankfurt
Offenbach
Mainz
Darmstadt
Würzburg

Somme
St. Quentin
Amiens
LUXEMBOURG
Trier
Kaiserslautern
Mannheim
Luxembourg
Ludwigshafen
Heidelberg
Thionville
Saarbrücken
2
Beauvais
Metz
Karlsruhe
Marne
Reims
Châlons-sur-Marne
Stuttgart
Paris
Nancy
lles
Seine
Troyes
Strasbourg
Rhine
VOSGES
rtres
Freiburg

Orléans
Montargis
Mulhouse
Lake
Constance
Winterthur
AUSTRIA
A N C E
Basel
Zürich
Vaduz
Dijon
Besançon
Luzern
LIECHTENSTEIN
3
Bourges
JURA MTS
Neuchâtel
Berne
Chur
Châteauroux
Chalon-sur-Saône
L. de
Neuchâtel
Fribourg
SWITZERLAND
Lausanne
Montluçon
Mâcon
Lake
Geneva
Montreux
Rhône
A L P S
Vichy
Loire
Saône
Geneva
Matterhorn
4477
Mt Rosa
4634
Lake
Como
Como
Bergamo
Clermont
Ferrand
Annecy
Mt. Blanc
4807
Novara
4
Milan
St. Etienne
Lyon
A
Allier
Mt. Dore
1886
Grenoble
L
Po
MASSIF
Le Puy
Turin
Asti
Mt. Mezenc
1754
Valence
Les Ecrins
4103
ITALY
10°
CENTRAL
Rhône
ALPES
Montélimar
8°

C É V E N N E S
Avignon
MARITIMES
Nîmes
Durance
MONACO
Montpellier
Arles
Aix-en-Provence
Cannes
Nice
Béziers
Marseille
5
Carcassonne
Gulf of Lions
Toulon
Narbonne
Îles d'Hyères
Perpignan
DORRA
M E D I T E R R A N E A N   S E A
2°
4°
6°

Corsica
J
5
Calvi
Bastia
Mt Cinto
2710
42°
Aleria
Ajaccio
6
at same scale

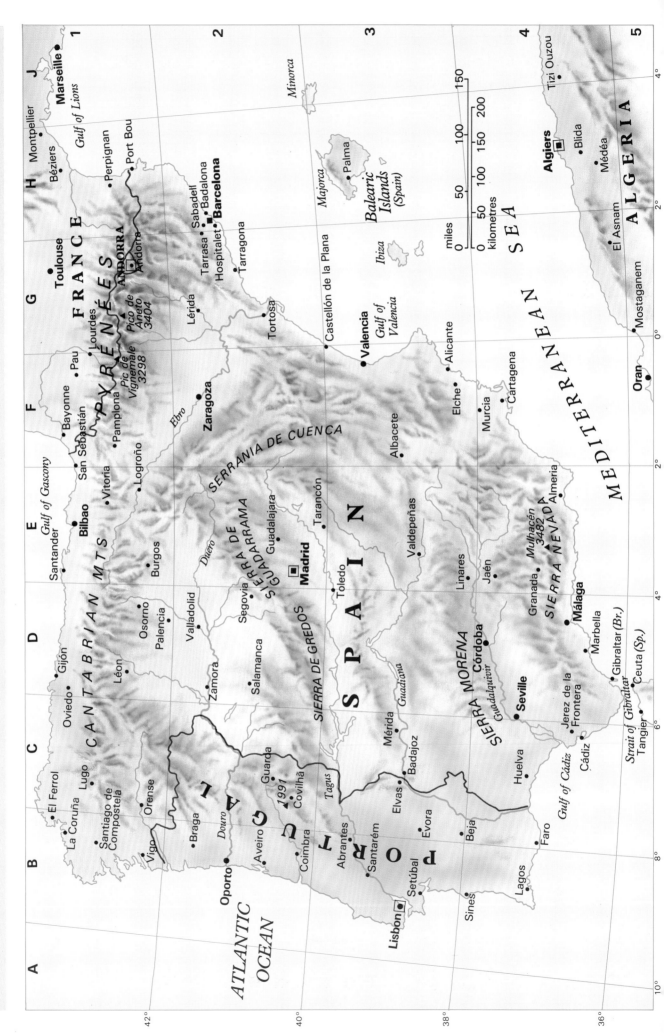

FRANCE

PYRÉNÉES

Marseille
Montpellier
Béziers
Gulf of Lions
Perpignan
Port Bou
Toulouse
Lourdes
Bayonne
Pau
Pic de Vignemale 3298
Pico de Aneto 3404
ANDORRA
Andorra
Barcelona
Badalona
Sabadell
Tarrasa
Hospitalet
Tarragona
Tortosa
Castellón de la Plana
Minorca
Majorca
Palma
Ibiza
Balearic Islands (Spain)
Bayonne
San Sebastián
Pamplona
Logroño
Vitoria
Lérida
Zaragoza
Ebro
SERRANIA DE CUENCA
Valencia
Gulf of Valencia
Alicante
Elche
Murcia
Cartagena
MEDITERRANEAN SEA
Gulf of Gascony
Santander
Bilbao
CANTABRIAN MTS
Burgos
Duero
Valladolid
Palencia
Osorno
Léon
Gijón
Oviedo
Lugo
Santiago de Compostela
La Coruña
El Ferrol
ATLANTIC OCEAN
Vigo
Oporto
Orense
Braga
Douro
Aveiro
Guarda
1991
Coimbra
Covilhã
PORTUGAL
Abrantes
Santarém
Tagus
Coimbra
Zamora
Salamanca
SIERRA DE GREDOS
SIERRA DE GUADARRAMA
Segovia
Guadalajara
Madrid
Tarancón
Toledo
SPAIN
Albacete
Valdepeñas
Linares
Jaén
SIERRA MORENA
Mérida
Badajoz
Guadiana
Córdoba
Guadalquivir
SIERRA NEVADA
Mulhacén 3482
Granada
Almeria
Málaga
Marbella
Gibraltar (Br.)
Ceuta (Sp.)
Strait of Gibraltar
Tangier
Cádiz
Gulf of Cádiz
Huelva
Seville
Jerez de la Frontera
Elvas
Évora
Beja
Faro
Lagos
Sines
Setúbal
Lisbon
P
ALGERIA
Tizi Ouzou
Algiers
Blida
Médéa
El Asnam
Mostaganem
Oran

miles
kilometres
0 50 100 150
0 50 100 150 200

1 2 3 4 5
J H G F E D C B A
4° 2° 0° 2° 4° 6° 8° 10°
42° 40° 38° 36°

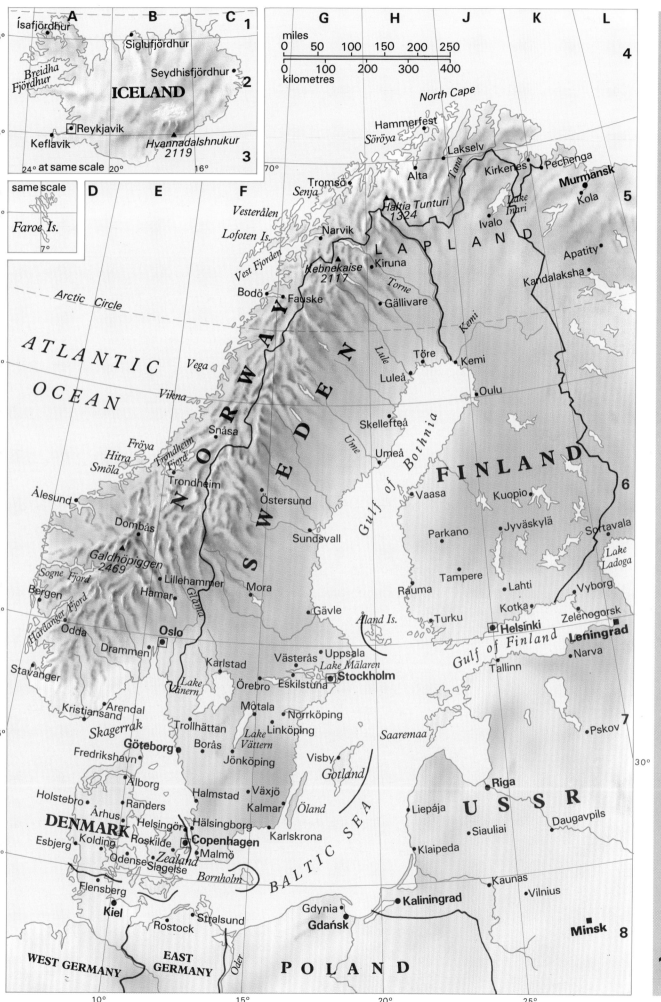

ICELAND

A1 Siglufjördhur
Ísafjördhur
Breidha Fjördhur
B2 Seydhisfjördhur
Reykjavik
Keflavik
Hvannadalshnukur 2119
24° at same scale 20° 16° 70°

same scale
Faroe Is.
7°

miles
0 50 100 150 200 250
0 100 200 300 400
kilometres

North Cape
Hammerfest
Söröya
Lakselv
Alta
Tromsö
Senja
Kirkenes Pechenga
Murmansk
Kola
Lake Inari
Ivalo
Haltia Tunturi 1324
LAPLAND
Narvik
Vesterålen
Lofoten Is.
Vest Fjorden
Kebnekaise 2117
Kiruna
Apatity
Kandalaksha
Bodö
Fauske
Torne
Gällivare
Arctic Circle
Kemi
Vega
Töre
Luleå
Kemi
Vikna
Oulu
Snåsa
Skellefteå
Fröya
Hitra
Smöla
Trondheim Fjord
Umeå
Gulf of Bothnia
FINLAND
Trondheim
Ålesund
Östersund
Vaasa
Kuopio
Sortavala
Dombås
Sundsvall
Parkano
Jyväskylä
Lake Ladoga
Galdhöpiggen 2469
Tampere
Lahti
Vyborg
Sogne Fjord
Bergen
Lillehammer
Mora
Rauma
Kotka
Zelenogorsk
Hamar
Gävle
Åland Is.
Turku
Helsinki
Leningrad
Hardanger Fjord
Odda
Oslo
Glama
Åland Is.
Gulf of Finland
Narva
Stavanger
Drammen
Karlstad
Västerås
Uppsala
Tallinn
Pskov
Kristiansand
Arendal
Lake Vänern
Örebro
Lake Mälaren
Eskilstuna
Stockholm
Skagerrak
Trollhättan
Motala
Norrköping
Saaremaa
Göteborg
Borås
Linköping
Fredrikshavn
Jönköping
Visby
Lake Vättern
Gotland
Riga
Ålborg
Halmstad
Växjö
USSR
Holstebro
Randers
Kalmar
Öland
Liepája
Daugavpils
Århus
Helsingör
Hälsingborg
Karlskrona
Siauliai
DENMARK
Roskilde
BALTIC SEA
Esbjerg
Kolding
Copenhagen
Malmö
Klaipeda
Odense
Zealand
Slagelse
Bornholm
Kaunas
Flensberg
Kiel
Kaliningrad
Vilnius
Rostock
Stralsund
Gdynia
Minsk
Gdańsk
WEST GERMANY
EAST GERMANY
Oder
POLAND

NORWAY
SWEDEN
ATLANTIC OCEAN

10° 15° 20° 25°
30°

CENTRAL EUROPE

A **B** **C** DENMARK **D** **E**

miles
0   50   100
0   50   100   150
kilometres

54°

NORTH SEA

Flensburg

Kiel

Neumünster

Stralsund

Rostock

Greifsw

West Frisian Is.

East Frisian Is.

Wadden Sea

Lübeck

Wismar

Schwerin

Neubrandenb

Groningen

Wilhelmshaven

Bremerhaven

Hamburg

Assen

Oldenburg

Bremen

Wittenberge

EAST

NETHERLANDS

WEST

Haarlem

Zwolle

Amsterdam

The Hague

Apeldoorn

Enschede

Utrecht

Osnabrück

Ems

Weser

Hanover

Wolfsburg

Potsdam

GERMAN

52°

Rotterdam

Arnhem

Münster

Bielefeld

Brunswick

Salzgitter

Magdeburg

Dordrecht

Maas

Gelsenkirchen

GERMANY

HARZ MTS

Elbe

Dessau

Eindhoven

Duisburg

Dortmund

Kassel

Halle

Lauchham

Antwerp

Essen

Bochum

Wuppertal

Weimar

Leipzig

Meissen

Brussels

Mönchen-Gladbach

Düsseldorf

Cologne

Erfurt

Gera

Dres

Maastricht

Aachen

Bonn

Siegen

Thuringian Forest

Karl Marx Stadt

Zwickau

BELGIUM

Liège

Wetzlar

Charleroi

Rhine

Fulda

ORE MT

Koblenz

Karlovy Va

ARDENNES

EIFEL

50°

Wiesbaden

Frankfurt

Bayreuth

Charleville-Mézières

LUXEMBOURG

Mosel

Offenbach

Main

Bamberg

Plzeň

Luxembourg

Mainz

Darmstadt

Würzburg

Bohemian Forest

Verdun

Thionville

Kaiserslautern

Mannheim

Fürth

Metz

Saarbrücken

Heidelberg

Nuremberg

Meuse

Regensburg

St. Dizier

Nancy

Karlsruhe

Danube

Strasbourg

Rhine

Stuttgart

FRANCE

Offenburg

Ulm

Augsburg

48°

VOSGES

Freiburg

Black Forest

Munich

Mulhouse

Memmingen

Salz

Lake Constance

Kempten

Inn

Dijon

Doubs

Basel

Winterthur

Besançon

Zürich

Zugspitze 2963

Innsbruck

Luzern

Lake Zürich

LIECHTENSTEIN

AU

Berne

Vaduz

Chur

Gross Glockne 3798

JURA MTS

L. de Neuchâtel

SWITZERLAND

ALPS

Merano

Lausanne

Saône

Lake Geneva

Jungfrau 4158

ITALY

Bolzano

Geneva

14

6°   8°   10°   12°

F   G   H   J   K

BALTIC SEA

Gulf of Gdańsk

Kaliningrad

Chernyakhovsk

U S S R

Kaunas

1

Gdynia

Gdańsk

Elbląg

Grodno

Kołobrzeg

Koszalin

Malbork

Olsztyn

Wolin

Chojnice

Szczecin

Łomża

Białystok

2

Stargard

Piła

Bydgoszcz

Toruń

Inowrocław

Włocławek

Pułtusk

Kostrzyn

P O L A N D

Warsaw

Siedlce

Brest

ankfurt

Oder

Poznań

Gubin

Leszno

Kalisz

Łódź

Vistula

ttbus

Neisse

Głogów

Radom

Lublin

Spree

Legnica

Wrocław

Görlitz

3

Zamość

Wałbrzych

Czestochowa

Liberec

SUDETEN MTS

Zabrze

sti nad Labem

Katowice

Chorzów

Prague

Krakow

Tarnow

Rzeszów

Przemyśl

Ostrava

C A R P A T H I A N M T S

CZECHOSLOVAKIA

Olomouc

Rysy 2499

Vltava

Jihlava

▲ Gerlachovka Stit
2655

4

Brno

Váh

Košice

Uzhgorod

Trěbǒn

Znojmo

Mukachevo

Gmünd

Krems

Miskolc

Linz

Bratislava

St. Polten

Vienna

Kékes 1015 ▲

Tisza

Satu
Mare

Lake
Neusiedler

Győr

Danube

Budapest

Debrecen

Leoben

H U N G A R Y

Oradea

5

R I A

Szombathely

Lake
Balaton

Graz

Kecskemet

genfurt

Maribor

Nagykanizsa

ROMANIA

Szeged

Arad

Pécs

16°   20°   22°

15

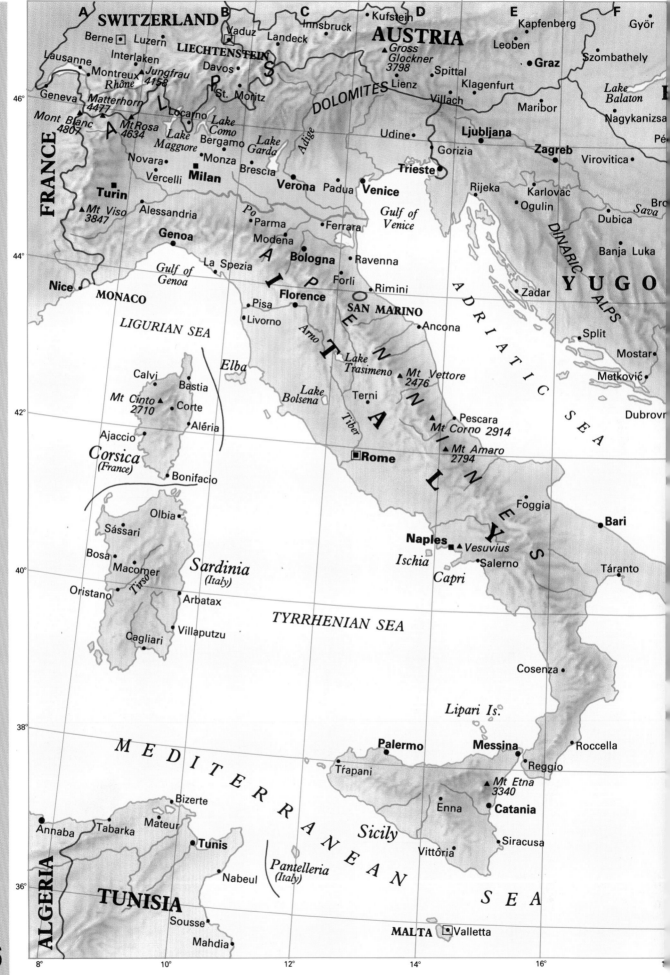

SWITZERLAND

Berne ◉ Luzern

AUSTRIA

• Kufstein

• Innsbruck

LIECHTENSTEIN

Vaduz ▣

Landeck

• Kapfenberg

• Leoben

Graz

• Szombathely

Lausanne

Interlaken

Montreux

Rhône

Jungfrau
4158

Davos

*Gross
Glockner*
3798

Spittal

Klagenfurt

Villach

*Lake
Balaton*

Geneva

Matterhorn
4477

St. Moritz

DOLOMITES

Lienz

Maribor

Nagykanizsa

Mont Blanc
4807

Mt Rosa
4634

Locarno

*Lake
Como*

Adige

Udine

Gorizia

Ljubljana

Zagreb

Virovitica

FRANCE

Lake
Maggiore

Bergamo

*Lake
Garda*

Verona Padua

Venice

Trieste

Rijeka

Karlovac

Ogulin

Sava

Dubica

Turin

Mt Viso
3847

Novara

Vercelli

Monza

Brescia

Milan

*Gulf of
Venice*

Y U G O

Alessandria

Po

Parma

Ferrara

Banja Luka

Genoa

Modena

Bologna

Ravenna

DINARIC

Zadar

*Gulf of
Genoa*

La Spezia

Forli

Rimini

Florence

SAN MARINO

Split

Nice

Pisa

MONACO

Livorno

Arno

A   P   E

*Lake
Trasimeno*

Ancona

Mostar

Metković

ADRIATIC

LIGURIAN SEA

Elba

*Lake
Bolsena*

Terni

Mt Vettore
2476

Dubrovn

Calvi

Bastia

Mt Corno 2914

Pescara

SEA

Mt Cinto
2710

Corte

Tiber

N   N   I

Mt Amaro
2794

Ajaccio

Aléria

▣**Rome**

Corsica
(France)

Bonifacio

Foggia

Olbia

L

Bari

Sássari

N

Naples

Vesuvius

Táranto

Bosa

Ischia

Salerno

Macomer

Sardinia
(Italy)

Capri

Oristano

Tirso

Arbatax

TYRRHENIAN SEA

Cagliari

Villaputzu

Cosenza

Lipari Is.

M

Palermo

Messina

Roccella

Trapani

Reggio

*Mt Etna
3340*

E

Bizerte

Enna

Catania

Annaba

Tabarka

Mateur

D

Siracusa

ALGERIA

Tunis

Sicily

Vittória

Nabeul

*Pantelleria
(Italy)*

TUNISIA

S

Sousse

MALTA ▣ Valletta

Mahdia

SEA

G   H   J   K   L   M   N

Botoşani

Satu Mare

■ Budapest

Iaşi

Kishinev • Tiraspol

1

Debrecen

Kecskemet

Oradea
• Dej

Cluj

Bacău

Odessa ■

CARPATHIAN MTS

N G A R Y

Szeged

Tirgu Mureş

Subotica

Arad

Alba Iulia

Mures

Timişoara

TRANSYLVANIAN ALPS

Braşov

Galaţi

Izmail

2

Sombor

Kikinda

Lugoj

Negoiu 2548

Brăila

Tulcea

jek

Zrenjanin

R O M A N I A

Novi Sad

Ploeşti

■ Belgrade

Turnu Severin

Piteşti

□ Bucharest

Constanţa

A V I A

Craiova

Danube

arajevo

Kragujevac

Caracal

Giurgiu

Silistra

Mangalia

Vidin

Ruse

Tolbukhin

Balchik

3

zla

Lom

Razgrad

Niš

Pleven

Vratsa

Varna

Leskovac

B U L G A R I A

Karnobat

BLACK SEA

Nikšić

Pec

Priština

K A N M T S

Stara
Zagora

Yambol

Burgas

Titograd

Sofia □

Plovdiv

otor

Bar

Shkodër

Skopje

Blagoevgrad

Maritsa

Kirklareli

Midye

Shëngjin

Titov Veles

RHODOPE MTS

Edirne

Luleburgaz

Istanbul ■

4

Durrës

Tiranë □

Petrich

Smolyan

Komotini

Tekirdağ

SEA OF
MARMARA

Elbasan

Ohridsko
Lake

Ohrid

Bitola

Kilkis

Sérrai

Xánthi

Alexandroúpolis

Kesan

Bandirma

Bursa

ALBANIA

Prespa
Lake

Edhessa

Thessaloniki

Thásos

Gallipoli

Çanakkale

Vlorë

Korçë

Kastoria

Samothráki

Imroz

T U R K E Y

Mt Olympus
2911

Limnos

5

Ioánnina

Lárisa

Vólos

AEGEAN

Ayvalik

Corfu

Igoumenítsa

Trikkala

Mitilíni

Bergama

Arta

Fársala

Lésvos

Manisa

Préveza

Lamía

Euboea

Skiros

Izmir

G R E E C E

Khalkis

Khíos

Mesolóngion

Návpaktos

Marathon

SEA

Aydin

Pátrai

Athens □

Ándros

Sámos

Söke

Corinth

Piraeus

Milâs

Kefallinia

Argos

Kéa

Tínos

Zákinthos

Pírgos

Návplion

Ikaria

6

Kíthnos

Náxos

Marmaris

Kalámai

Milos

Kos

Pílos

Thíra

Rhodes

Ráthimnon

Kíthira

SEA OF CRETE

Rhodes

Lindos

7

IONIAN
SEA

Kárpathos

Canea

Crete

Iráklion

miles
0   50   100   150

kilometres
0 50 100 150 200

20°   22°   24°   26°   28°

17

60° 70° 80°

A B C D E

A R C T I C

Franz Josef Land

0°

NORWAY

SWEDEN

FINLAND

Oslo ◻

DENMARK

Copenhagen ◻

Stockholm ◻

BALTIC SEA

Helsinki ◻

Murmansk

BARENTS SEA

Kolguyev

Novaya
Zemlya

Severna
Zemly

KARA
SEA

Taym

20°

POLAND

Warsaw ◻

Kaliningrad

Grodno

Tallinn

Novgorod

Riga

Pskov

Vitebsk

Leningrad

Lake Ladoga

White
Sea

Petrozavodsk

Lake
Onega

Arkhangel'sk

Dvina

Syktyvkar

Salekhard

Narodnaya
1894

No

50°

Lvov

Brest

Vilnius

Minsk

Gomel

Bryansk

Kalinin

Yaroslavl'

Cherepovets

Vologda

Kirov

Berezniki

S

West
Siberian
Plain

Yenisei

Rovno

Dnieper

Ryazan

Moscow ◻

Kostroma

Izhevsk

U

Serov

N I O N   O F   S O V I E

Ob

Kishinev

Vinnitsa

Kiev

Sumy

Kursk

Orel

Tula

Ul'yanovsk

Gorki

Cheboksary

Perm

N

Nizhniy Tagil

Dnepropetrovsk

Zaporozhye

Kharkov

Voronezh

Tambov

Saratov

Penza

Kazan

Ufa

R

Sverdlovsk

Tyumen

Odessa

Krivoy
Rog

Kherson

Zhdanov

Donetsk

Rostov

Taganrog

Engels

Tol'yatti

Kuybyshev

Chelyabinsk

A

Kurgan

Omsk

Tomsk

Ach

Simferopol'

Krasnodar

Don

Volga

Orenburg

Magnitogorsk

Kustanay

Petropavlovsk

L

Novosibirsk

Kemer

BLACK
SEA

Ordzhonikidze

Stavropol'

Volgograd

Ural

Ural'sk

Aktyubinsk

Orsk

U

Prokopyevsk

Novokuznetsk

40°

40°

TURKEY

Batumi

Elbrus
5633

CAUCASUS
MTS

Groznyy

Astrakhan

Guryev

Pavlodar

Irtysh

Semipalatinsk

Barnaul

A L T A

Tbilisi

Makhachkala

Yerevan

Mt. Ararat
5165

Tabriz

CASPIAN SEA

ARAL
SEA

Karaganda

Mt. Belukha
4506

NAGROS MTS

ELBURZ MTS

Baku

Syr Darya

Lake
Balkhash

30°

Tehran ◻

IRAN

Mashhad

Esfahan

Ashkhabad

Amu Darya

Chardzhou

Bukhara

Chimkent

Leninabad

Tashkent

Frunze

Alma-Ata

Urum

Samarkand

Andizhan

Osh

Hantengri Feng
7439

Dushanbe

Communism Peak
7495

AFGHANISTAN

60° 80°

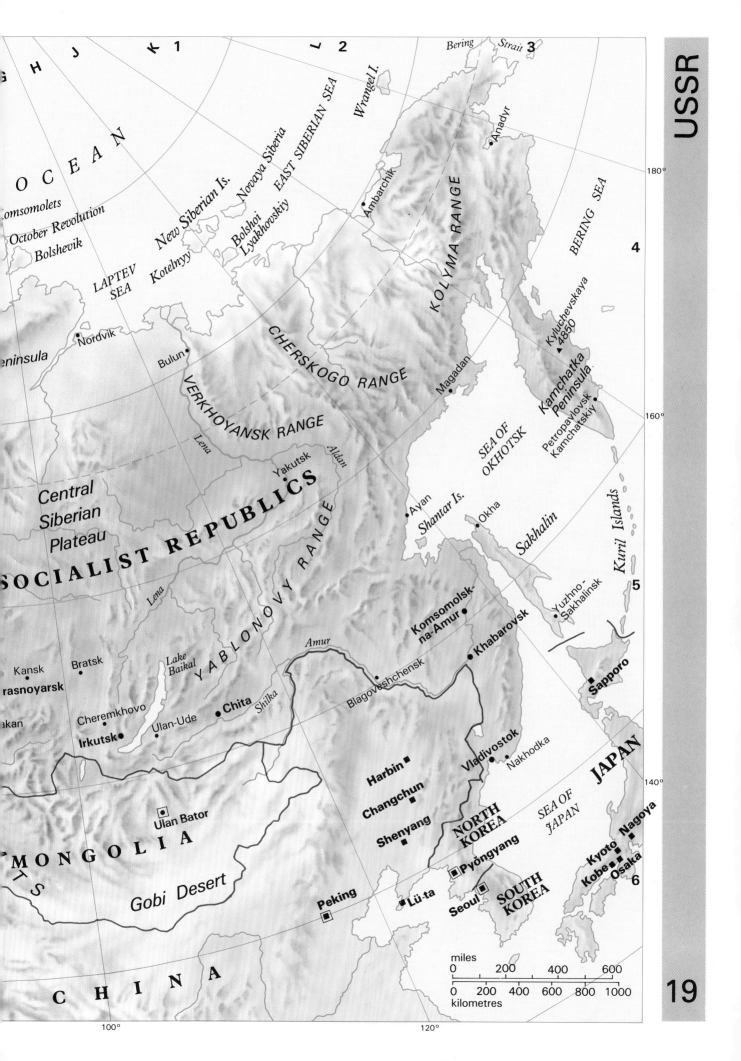

G H J K **1** L **2** Bering *Strait* **3**

O C E A N

Komsomolets

October Revolution

Bolshevik

New Siberian Is.

Novaya Siberia

Bolshoi Lyakhovskiy

EAST SIBERIAN SEA

Wrangel I.

LAPTEV SEA

Kotelnyy

• Ambarchik

KOLYMA RANGE

BERING SEA

• Anadyr

180°

4

Peninsula

• Nordvik

CHERSKOGO RANGE

Kyluchevskaya 4850 ▲

• Bulun

VERKHOYANSK RANGE

• Magadan

Kamchatka Peninsula

160°

Lena

• Yakutsk

Aldan

SEA OF OKHOTSK

Petropavlovsk Kamchatskiy •

Central Siberian Plateau

SOCIALIST REPUBLICS

• Ayan

Shantar Is.

• Okha

Sakhalin

Kuril Islands

Lena

YABLONOVY RANGE

Yuzhno-Sakhalinsk •

5

Komsomolsk-na-Amur •

Amur

Kansk • Bratsk •

Lake Baikal

• **Khabarovsk**

rasnoyarsk

Cheremkhovo •

Ulan-Ude • • **Chita**

Shilka

Blagoveshchensk •

■ **Sapporo**

Irkutsk •

Vladivostok •

• Nakhodka

JAPAN

140°

Harbin ■

□ Ulan Bator

Changchun ■

NORTH KOREA

SEA OF JAPAN

MONGOLIA

Shenyang ■

Gobi Desert

□ **Pyŏngyang**

Kyoto ■ ■ **Nagoya**

Kobe ■ ■ **Osaka**

6

Peking □

• **Lü-ta**

Seoul □ **SOUTH KOREA**

C H I N A

miles
0   200   400   600

0   200   400   600   800 1000
kilometres

100°   120°

19

THE MIDDLE EAST

20

Edirne **A** **Istanbul** **B** Sinop **C** Batumi **D** **E**
Gallipoli *Sea of* Izmit BLACK SEA **Tbilisi** Kirovabad
Marmara Adapazari Samsun PONTINE MTS **Yerevan**
Bursa **Ankara** Sivas Erzurum *Mt Ararat* 5165
Eskisehir *Kizil* Mt Ararat
T U R K E Y Kayseri Malatya Diyarbakir **Tabriz**
Izmir Afyon *Lake Tuz* Mt Erciyas Maras Mardin Siirt *Lake Van* *Lake Urmia* Ra
Konya 3916 *Lake Urmia* **Maragheh**
Rhodes **TAURUS MTS** **Adana** Urfa Rezaiyeh
Mersin **Gaziantep** Erbil **Qaz**
Antakya **Halab** **Mosul** Kirkuk
CYPRUS Latakia Hamadan
◻ Nicosia Hama **S Y R I A** **Qahremanshah**
MEDITERRANEAN Tripoli **Homs** *Euphrates* *Tharthar*
SEA **Beirut** ◻ **Basin** *Tigris* **I R A Q** ◻ **Baghdad** Khorramaba
LEBANON ◻ **Damascus**
Haifa Irbid *Syrian* Karbala Hilla
Matruh **Tel-Aviv-Yafo** Zarqa *Desert* An Najaf **Ahvaz**
Alexandria **ISRAEL** ◻ **Amman** *Hor al* Khorrams
El Mahalla el Kubra Port Said Jerusalem *Hammar*
Tanta **El Mansura** *Dead Sea* **JORDAN** **Basra** **Abad**
El Giza ◻ *Suez Canal* Elat Al Jawf **KUWAIT** ◻ Kuwait
Cairo Suez
Beni Suef *Gebel Katherina* *An Nafud* Hafar
El Minya *Gulf of Suez* 2637 Tabuk Al Khu
Asyût *Hail*
E G Y P T *Nile* Luxor **H** **Ramah** Ho
Aswân **E** Medina ◻
Lake **J** **Riyadh**
Nasser Yanbu'al Bahr **A** **S A U D I**
Wadi Halfa *Nubian* **Z** **A R A B I A**
Dongola *Desert* **R** Jiddah **Mecca**
E At Tā'if
D **A**
S U D A N Port Sudan **S** *Rub* al
Suakin **I**
R
Jizân
S
E
Khartoum North **A**
Omdurman ◻ **Khartoum** Kassala Massawa **YEMEN** Hodeida
Wad Medani Asmara **Sana** ◻ **SOUTH**
YEMEN
Sennar **ETHIOPIA** Taizz
Hodeida **Muk**
◻ **Aden**

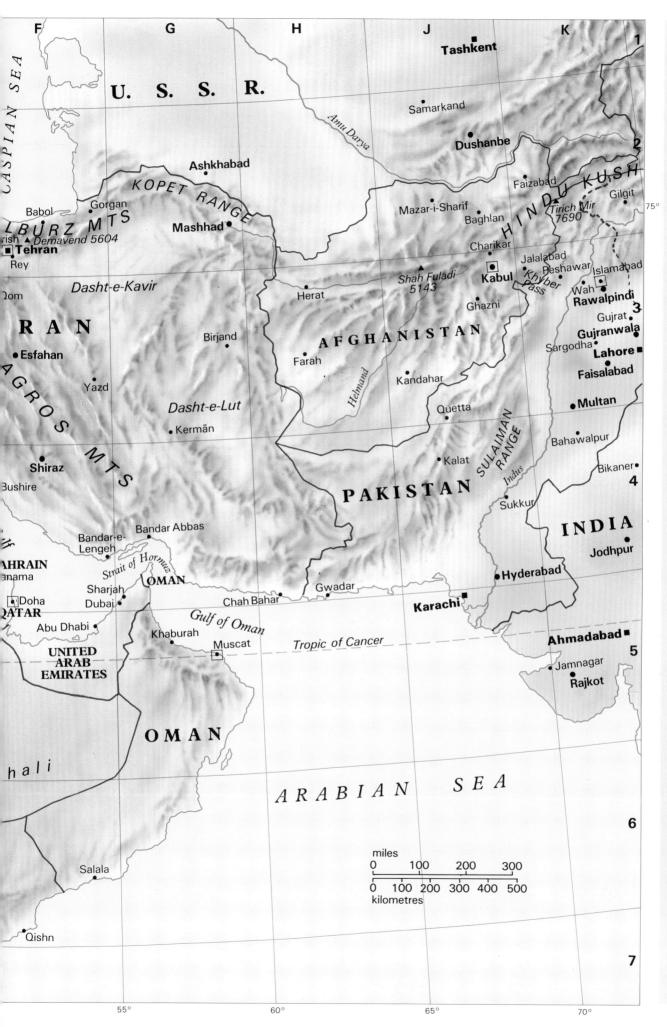

F   G   H   J   K

CASPIAN SEA

U. S. S. R.

1

Tashkent

Samarkand

Amu Darya

Dushanbe

Ashkhabad

KOPET RANGE

2

Faizabad

Babol Gorgan

LBURZ MTS

Mazar-i-Sharif

HINDU KUSH

Gilgit

rish ▲ *Demavend 5604*

Mashhad

Baghlan

▲ *Tirich Mir 7690*

75°

■ **Tehran**

Rey

Charikar

Jalalabad

Peshawar

Islamabad ☐

Dasht-e-Kavir

Herat

▲ *Shah Fuladi 5143*

☐ **Kabul**

Khyber Pass

Wah ■

Rawalpindi

3

Qom

I R A N

Esfahan

Birjand

AFGHANISTAN

Ghazni

Gujrat

Gujranwala

Sargodha

Lahore ■

Yazd

Farah

Kandahar

Faisalabad

Dasht-e-Lut

Helmand

Quetta

Multan

ZAGROS MTS

Kermān

Bahawalpur

Shiraz

Kalat

SULAIMAN RANGE

Bikaner ■

4

Bushire

PAKISTAN

Indus

Sukkur

I N D I A

Jodhpur

Bandar Abbas

Bandar-e-Lengeh

Strait of Hormuz

BAHRAIN

anama

OMAN

Hyderabad

AHRAIN

Sharjah

Gwadar

☐ **Doha**

Dubai

Chah Bahar

Karachi ■

QATAR

Abu Dhabi

Gulf of Oman

Khaburah

Tropic of Cancer

Ahmadabad ■

5

UNITED ARAB EMIRATES

Muscat ☐

Jamnagar

Rajkot

O M A N

h a l i

A R A B I A N   S E A

6

Salala

miles

0   100   200   300

0 100 200 300 400 500

kilometres

Qishn

7

55°   60°   65°   70°

A **B** **C** **D**

35°

Herat

HINDU KUSH

KARAKORAM RANGE

Gilgit

Charikar

Jalalabad

Kabul

Khyber Pass

Peshawar

Nanda Parbat 8126

K2 8611

Karakoram Pass

Leh

Birjand

AFGHANISTAN

Ghazni

Wah

Islamabad

Srinagar

Rawalpindi

Indus

Farah

Helmand

Jammu

Sialkot

Gujrat

H

Kandahar

Sargodha

Gujranwala

30°

Lahore

Amritsar

Faisalabad

Jullundur

Quetta

Sahiwal

Ludhiana

Chandigarh

Nanda De 781

Multan

Patiala

Dehra Dun

Ambala

Kalat

SULAIMAN RANGE

PAKISTAN

Bahawalpur

Saharanpur

Rohtak

Meerut

Moradabad

Silg

IRAN

Indus

Delhi

Rampur

Bikaner

New Delhi

Bareilly

Sukkur

Aligarh

Shahjahan

Khairpur

Alwar

Agra

Mathura

Lucknow

Chah Bahar

Ajmer

Jaipur

25°

Jodhpur

Gwalior

Kanpur

Gwadar

Thar Desert

Kota

Jhansi

Allahab

Hyderabad

Udaipur

Tropic of Cancer

I N D

Karachi

Ahmadabad

Ratlam

Ujjain

Bhopal

Jabalp

Jamnagar

Indore

Rajkot

Vadodara

Bhavnagar

Surat

Jalgaon

Nagpur

Raip

20°

Gulf of Cambay

Malegaon

Akola

Nasik

Nander

Bombay

Ahmadnagar

60°

A R A B I A N   S E A

Pune

D e c c a n

Warangal

Godava

Sholapur

Hyderabad

Vijayaw

Kolhapur

Guntur

15°

Belgaum

Kurnool

Machilipatna

WESTERN

Hubli

EASTERN GHATS

Nellore

GHATS

Mangalore

Bangalore

Madra

Mysore

10°

Salem

Cuddalore

Calicut

Coimbatore

Tiruchirappa

Lakshadweep Is. (India)

Cochin

Alleppey

Madurai

Jaffna

Tuticorin

Trivandrum

Trincomalee

Nagercoil

SRI LANKA

Colombo

Galle

miles

0   100   200   300   400

0   100   200   300   400   500   600

kilometres

65°   70°   75°   80°

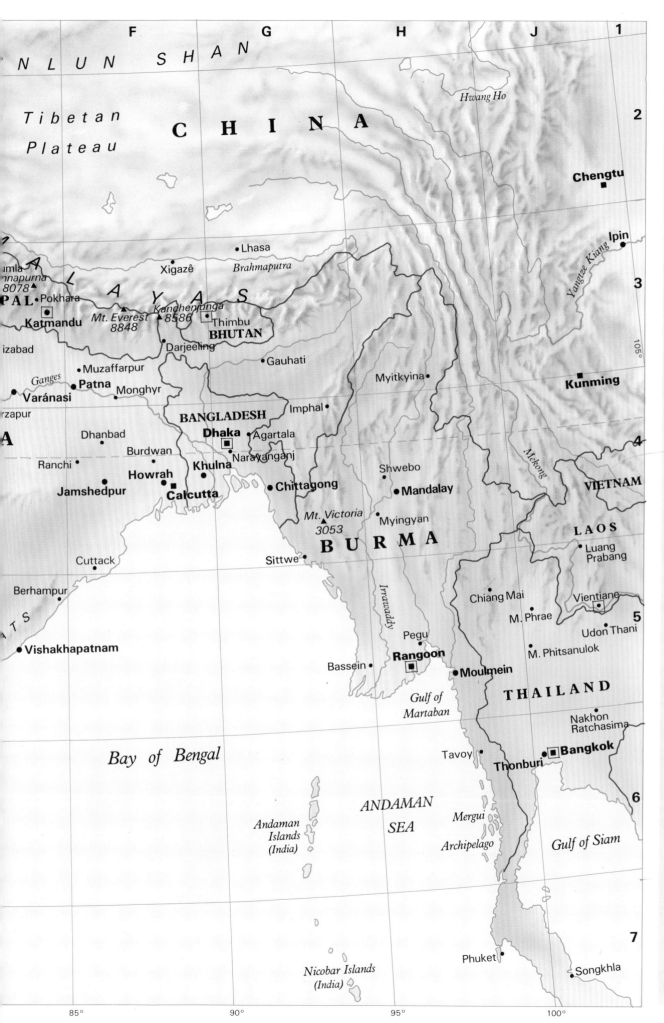

F   G   H   J   1

NLUN SHAN

Tibetan   CHINA   2
Plateau   *Hwang Ho*

                                                              Chengtu ■   2

                                                                              Ipin ■
M   • Lhasa   *Yangtze Kiang*
nnapurna Xigazê   *Brahmaputra*   3
8078 ▲   Kanchenjunga   105°
PAL • Pokhara   *L A Y A S* 8586 □ Thimbu
Katmandu ◉ *Mt. Everest* ▲ **BHUTAN**
izabad   8848   • Darjeeling
                              • Gauhati   Myitkyina •
• Muzaffarpur   **Kunming** ■
Ganges **Patna** Monghyr   Imphal •
Varánasi   *Mekong*
rzapur   **BANGLADESH** • Agartala   4
A   Dhanbad **Dhaka** ◉   Shwebo •   **VIETNAM**
         Burdwan   Narayanganj
• Ranchi **Howrah** **Khulna**   • **Mandalay**   **LAOS**
Jamshedpur **Calcutta** ◼ **Chittagong**   • Luang
                              Mt. Victoria • Myingyan   Prabang
• Cuttack   ▲ 3053   Chiang Mai • Vientiane □
                              B U R M A   • M. Phrae 5
• Berhampur   Sittwe •   *Irrawaddy*   Udon Thani •
                                                              • M. Phitsanulok
Vishakhapatnam   Pegu •
T S   **Rangoon** ◉   **T H A I L A N D**
                                    Bassein • • **Moulmein**
                                                              Nakhon
                                    Gulf of   Ratchasima •
                                    Martaban
                    Bay of Bengal   Tavoy • **Thonburi** ◉ **Bangkok**

                                                                              6
                              ANDAMAN
                    Andaman *SEA*   *Mergui*
                    Islands   *Archipelago* *Gulf of Siam*
                    (India)

                                                                              7

                    Nicobar Islands   Phuket •   • Songkhla
                    (India)

85°   90°   95°   100°

23

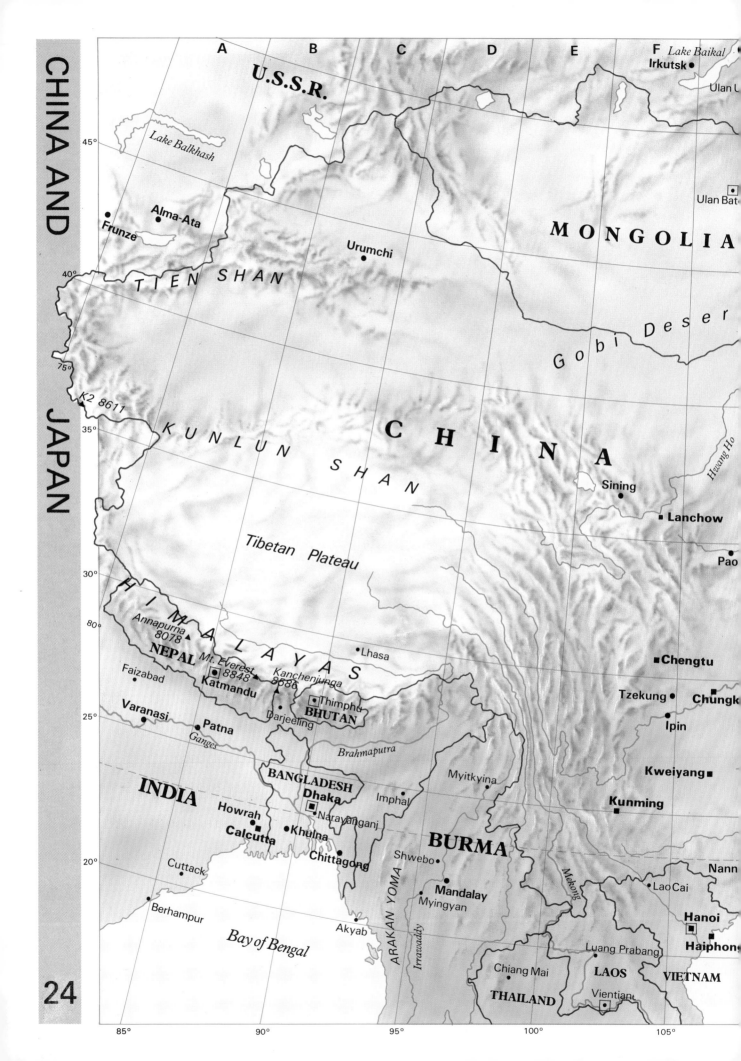

A   B   C   D   E   F

45°

Lake Baikal

Irkutsk ●

Ulan U

□ Ulan Bat

M O N G O L I A

Lake Balkhash

40°

● **Alma-Ata**

Frunze ●

T I E N   S H A N

Urumchi ●

G o b i   D e s e r

75°

K2 8611

35°

K U N L U N   S H A N

C H I N A

Sining ●

■ **Lanchow**

Tibetan Plateau

Pao ●

30°

80°

H

I *Annapurna*
8078 ▲

M

NEPAL

A

L

● **Lhasa**

Faizabad ●

Mt. Everest
□ *8848* ▲ *Kanchenjunga*
Katmandu   *8586*

A

Y   ▲

Darjeeling □ *Thimphu*

A

BHUTAN

Chengtu ■

Tzekung ●

Chungk

25°

Varanasi

● **Patna**

Ganges

Brahmaputra

Ipin ●

BANGLADESH

Dhaka
□

Myitkyina ●

Kweiyang ■

INDIA

Howrah ●

■ **Calcutta**

● **Khulna**

Narayanganj

Imphal ●

BURMA

Kunming ■

Chittagong

20°

Cuttack ●

Shwebo ●

A R A K A N   Y O M A

Mekong

Nann

Lao Cai ●

Berhampur ●

Mandalay ●

Myingyan

Hanoi ■
□

Irrawaddy

Akyab ●

Bay of Bengal

Luang Prabang ●

Haiphon

Chiang Mai ●

LAOS

VIETNAM

THAILAND

Vientiane
□

85°   90°   95°   100°   105°

Hwang Ho

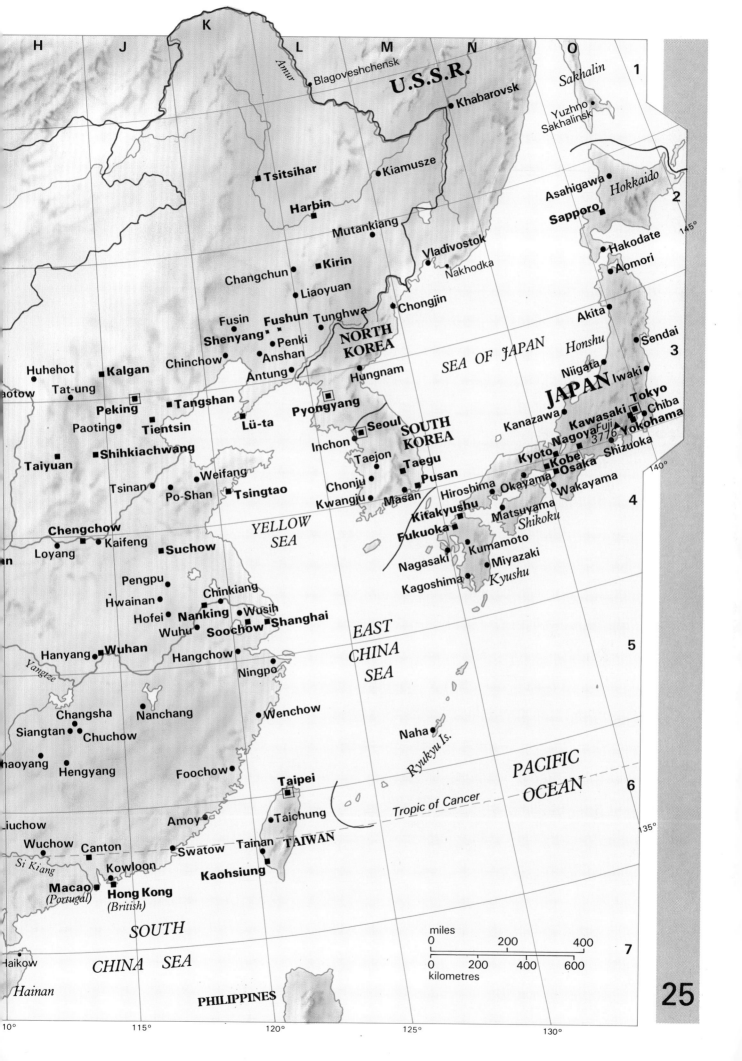

A   B   R. Red   C   D   E

- Shwebo
- **Mandalay**
- Myingyan

R. Irrawaddy

Salween

BURMA

- Pegu
- **Rangoon**
- **Moulmein**

- Tavoy

- Chiang Mai
- Vientiane
- Udon Thani

THAILAND

- Nakhon Sawan
- Nakhon Ratchasima
- **Bangkok**

- Luang Prabang

R. Mekong

VIETNAM

- Vinh

- Hué

- LaoCai

- Nanning

CHINA

- Haikou

Hainan

- **Canton**
- **Kowloon**
- **Macao** *(Portugal)*
- **Hong Kong** *(Britain)*

- **Hanoi**
- **Haiphong**

LAOS

- Ubon Ratchathani
- Pakse

- Attopeu

ANNAM HIGHLANDS

- **Da Nang**

- Qui Nhon

- Sisophon
- Battambang

KAMPUCHEA

- Kratie

Tonle Sap

Gulf of Siam

- Phnom Penh

- Kampot
- My Tho
- Rach Gia
- Can Tho

- Nha Trang
- Cam Ranh

- **Ho Chi-Minh City**

SOUTH CHINA SEA

- Swatow
- Tainan
- **Kaohsiu**

- Chi

- Lac

- Bag

Min

Palawan

SUL

SEA

- Phuket
- Trang
- Songkhla
- Kota Baharu
- Banda Aceh
- George Town
- Ipoh

Simeulue

Nias

Siberut

MALAYSIA

- **Medan**
- Pematangsiantar

Lake Toba

- **Kuala Lumpur**
- Gemas
- Johor Baharu
- **Singapore**

- Pakanbaru

- Padang
- Jambi

Kerintji 3805 ▲

BARISAN RANGE

Sumatra

- **Palembang**

- Kudat
- Kota Kinabalu

- **Bandar Seri Begawan**
- **BRUNEI**

Sabah

- Tawau

Murud 2438 ▲

Sarawak

- Sibu

- Kuching

- Pontianak
- Sintang

Borneo

- Samarinda
- Balikpapan

Makassar Strait

- Majene
- *Rantekombo 345*
- Watampon

Bangka

Belitung

- **Banjarmasin**

- **Ujung Pandang**

- Tanjungkarang

JAVA SEA

INDON

- ▣ **Jakarta**
- Bogor
- **Bandung**
- Semarang
- Surakarta
- Yogyakarta
- Kediri
- Malang
- **Surabaya**

Java

Lombok

Bali

Sumbawa

FLORES

Lesser Su

- Raba

- Waingap

- Suml

INDIAN OCEAN

20° · 15° · 10° · 5° · 95° · 0° · 5° · 10°

100°   105°   110°   115°

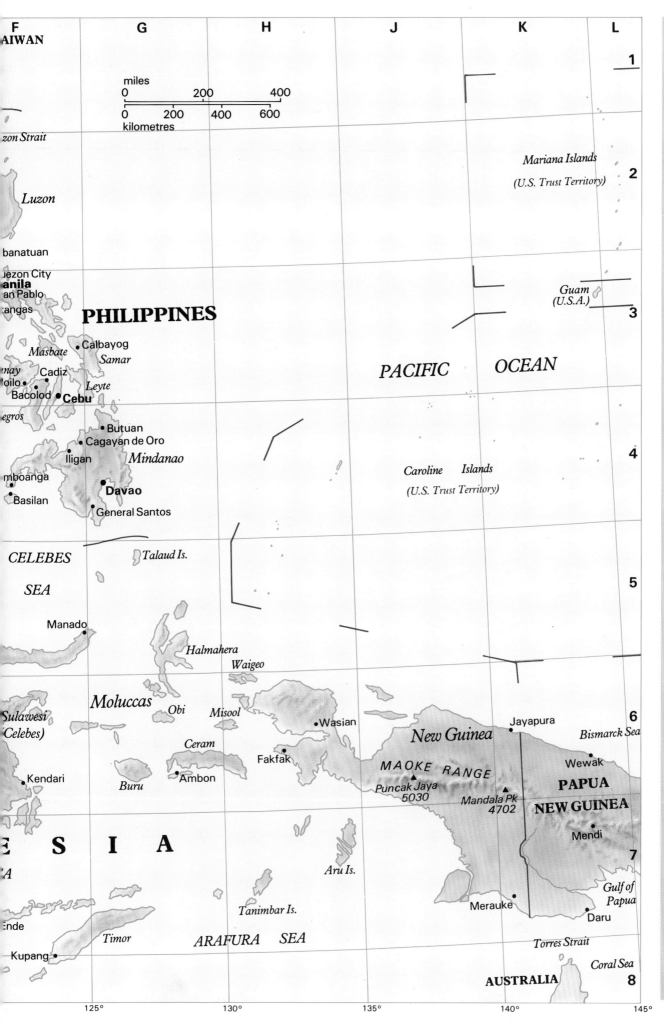

F G H J K L

1

miles
0   200   400
0   200   400   600
kilometres

Mariana Islands
(*U.S. Trust Territory*)

2

TAIWAN

zon Strait

Luzon

banatuan

uezon City
anila
an Pablo
angas

PHILIPPINES

Guam
(*U.S.A.*)

3

PACIFIC   OCEAN

•Calbayog
Masbate
Samar

nay Cadiz
oilo   *Leyte*
Bacolod   **Cebu**

egros

•Butuan
•Cagayan de Oro
Iligan   *Mindanao*

Davao

•General Santos

4

Caroline   Islands

(*U.S. Trust Territory*)

mboanga
•Basilan

CELEBES

SEA

•Manado

Talaud Is.

5

Halmahera
Waigeo

6

Moluccas   *Obi*   *Misool*   •Wasian

Sulawesi
(*Celebes*)

Ceram

Fakfak•

•Kendari

Buru   •Ambon

New Guinea   •Jayapura   *Bismarck Sea*

MAOKE   RANGE
▲   •Wewak
Puncak Jaya
5030   ▲
Mandala Pk   **PAPUA**
4702   **NEW GUINEA**

E   S   I   A

Aru Is.

•Mendi

7

Tanimbar Is.

•Merauke

Gulf of
Papua

•Daru

nde

Timor   *ARAFURA   SEA*

Torres Strait

Kupang

Coral Sea

AUSTRALIA   8

125°   130°   135°   140°   145°

27

A   B   C   D

Madeira

Tangier Ceuta Oran   **Algiers**
Kenitra **Tetuan** Sidi-bel-Abb. Blid
Rabat   **Fez** Tlemcen
Casablanca **Meknês** **Oujda**

30°

Safi
MOROCCO   **HIGH** **ATLAS** **SAHARAN ATLAS** Ghardaï
Marrakesh

Canary Is.

ALGERIA

Las Palmas

El Aaiún

Tropic of Cancer

20°

Nouadhibou

S   a   h

MAURITANIA   **MALI**

Nouakchott   Timbuktu
               Niger Gao

Cape Verde Is.

ATLANTIC

SENEGAL   Niamey
Dakar   Sok
   GAMBIA *Sénégal*
Banjul   **Bamako** Ouagadougou

OCEAN

Bissau **GUINEA**   **BURKINA FASO**
GUINEA BISSAU   Bobo-Dioulasso **BENIN**
      Kankan   *Volta* Ilori

10°

Conakry   Tamale **TOGO** Ogbomosho
Freetown **IVORY** **GHANA** Ibadan Osho
SIERRA LEONE Bouaké **Kumasi** **Abeokuta** Onits
    LIBERIA **COAST**   Lome Porto **Lagos**
Monrovia   Novo
Abidjan Sekondi- **Accra** Port Harc
     Takoradi

miles
0   400   800
0 400 800 1200
kilometres

EQUATOR
Gulf of Guinea   0°

30°   20°   10°   0° *São T*

K   L   M   N   P

Namib Windhoek   **BOTSWANA** Beitbridge
Walvis   *Kalahari* Louis Trichardt
Bay *Tropic of Capricorn* *Desert* Pietersburg 8

Desert   Gaborone

25° **NAMIBIA**   **Pretoria**   **Maputo**
             Mafikeng **Johannesburg** Mbabane
               Krugersdorp Benoni
             Vryburg Soweto Springs
             Potchefstroom Germiston **SWAZILAND**
             Vaal Vereeniging 9
        Upington Welkom Kroonstad
       Orange Kimberley
             Bloemfontein Maseru Pietermaritzburg
30°   **LESOTHO** **Durban**

REPUBLIC OF   *D R A K E N S B E R*
SOUTH AFRICA

       Beaufort West Queenstown
miles
0   200
0 200 400
kilometres

Paarl Ladysmith Grahamstown East London 10
Cape Town Worcester Oudtshoorn **Port Elizabeth**
Cape of Good Hope Mossel Bay

15°   20°   25°   30°   35°

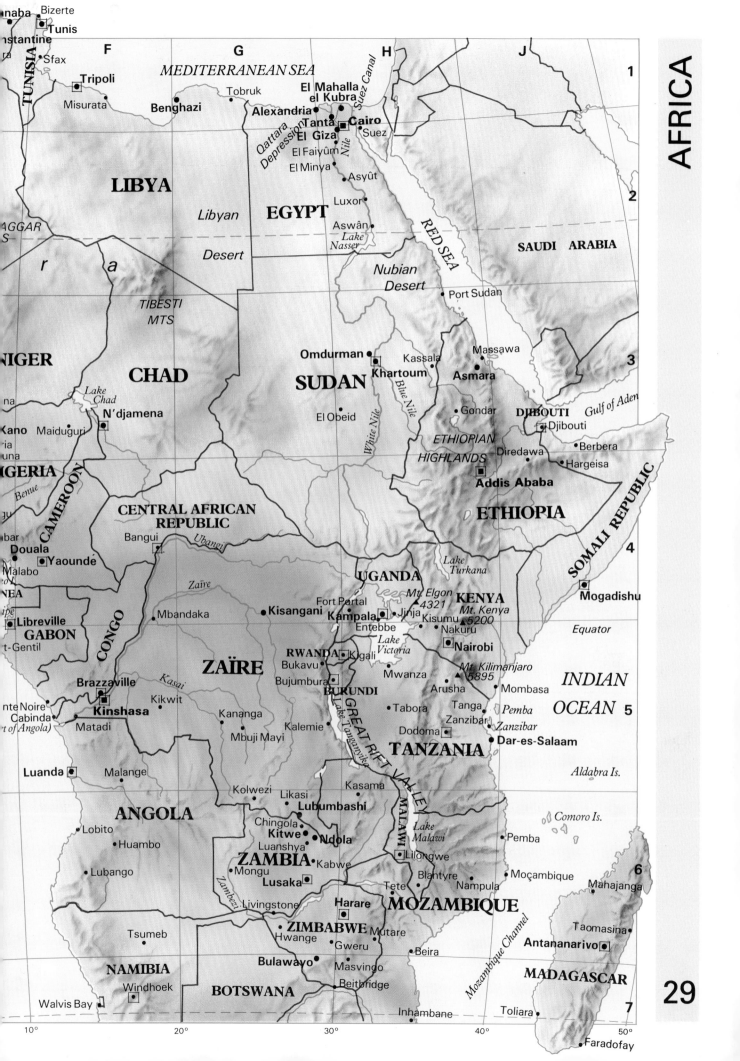

MEDITERRANEAN SEA

F

G

H

J

1

2

naba Bizerte
● Tunis
●
stantine ● Sfax
TUNISIA

● Tripoli
Misurata ●

● Tobruk

Benghazi ●

LIBYA

Libyan

Desert

AGGAR
S

r   a

TIBESTI
MTS

CHAD

NIGER

na

Lake
Chad

● N'djamena

Kano ● Maiduguri ●

ria
una

NIGERIA

Benue

CAMEROON

Douala ●
● Yaounde

Malabo
O l

NEA

ipe

● Libreville
GABON

t-Gentil

CONGO

Brazzaville ■

nte Noire ●
● Cabinda
rt of Angola)

● Kinshasa
Matadi ●

Luanda ■

Malange ●

ANGOLA

Lobito ●

● Huambo

● Lubango

Tsumeb ●

NAMIBIA

Windhoek ■

Walvis Bay ●

Qattara
Depression
El Mahalla
el Kubra
Alexandria ●
Tanta ● Cairo
El Gîza ● ● Suez
El Faiyûm ●
El Minya ●
● Asyût

EGYPT

Luxor ●

Aswân ●
Lake
Nasser

Nubian
Desert

Omdurman ●
SUDAN
Khartoum ■
● El Obeid

White Nile

Blue Nile

Suez Canal

Nile

RED SEA

● Port Sudan

Kassala ●

SAUDI ARABIA

3

● Massawa

Asmara ●

● Gondar

DJIBOUTI

Gulf of Aden

● Djibouti

● Berbera

ETHIOPIAN
HIGHLANDS Diredawa ●

CENTRAL AFRICAN
REPUBLIC

Bangui ■

Ubangi

Zaïre

● Kisangani
Mbandaka ●

ZAÏRE

Kikwit ●

Kasai

Kananga ●

Mbuji Mayi ●

Kolwezi ●

● Likasi
● Lubumbashi

Chingola ●
Kitwe ● ● Ndola
Luanshya ●
ZAMBIA ● Kabwe
Mongu ●
Lusaka ■

Zambezi

Livingstone ●

● Hargeisa

● Addis Ababa

ETHIOPIA

SOMALI REPUBLIC

■ Mogadishu

UGANDA Mt Elgon
Fort Portal ● ▲4321 KENYA
Kampala ■ ● Jinja Mt Kenya
Kisumu ● ▲5200
Entebbe ● Nakuru ●
RWANDA ■ Kigali
Bukavu ● Lake ● Nairobi
Bujumbura ■ Victoria
BURUNDI Mwanza ● Mt. Kilimanjaro
▲5895
Arusha ●
● Tabora Tanga ●
Dodoma ● Zanzibar ●
TANZANIA ● Dar-es-Salaam

Lake
Turkana

Equator

INDIAN

OCEAN

4

5

Mombasa ●

Pemba ●
Zanzibar

Aldabra Is.

Kasama ●

GREAT RIFT VALLEY

Lake Tanganyika

MALAWI

Lake
Malawi

Lilongwe ●

● Pemba

Comoro Is.

6

Harare ■

● Blantyre
Tete ●
Mutare ●

Nampula ●

● Moçambique

Mahajanga ●

ZIMBABWE
Hwange ●

Bulawayo ●

Masvingo ●

● Gweru

BOTSWANA Beitbridge ●

MOZAMBIQUE

● Beira

Mozambique Channel

● Taomasina

Antananarivo ■

MADAGASCAR

7

Inhambane ●

Toliara ●

Faradofay ●

10°   20°   30°   40°   50°

29

65°   70°

ALASKA RANGE
Mt. McKinley
6194

Yukon

Fairbanks

ALASKA (U.S.A.)

150°

Anchorage

Seward

Dawson

YUKON

MACKENZIE MTS

BEAUFORT
SEA

Melville I.

Banks I.

Viscount Melv
Sound

Amundsen
Gulf

Prince of
Wales I.

Mc Clure Strait

Mc Clintock
Channel

Victoria
Island

Gulf of Alaska

Mt. Logan
6050

Whitehorse

Skagway

Juneau

140°

PACIFIC

OCEAN

Queen
Charlotte Is.

Mackenzie

Coppermine

Great Bear
Lake

Bathurst Inlet

NORTHWEST
TERRITORIES

Yellowknife

Fort Reliance

Great
Slave Lake

Eskimo Poi

COASTAL MTS

ROCKY MOUNTAINS

SELKIRK MTS

Fort St. John

Prince George

BRITISH
COLUMBIA

ALBERTA

Edmonton

SASKATCHEWAN

C A N

Churchi

Vancouver I.

130°

Vancouver

Calgary

Saskatoon

Saskatchewan

Lake
Winnipeg

MANITOBA

45°

Seattle

Tacoma

Spokane

Mt. St. Helens

WASHINGTON

Portland

Salem

Lethbridge

Moose Jaw

Regina

Brandon

Winnipeg

Ken

OREGON

Snake

IDAHO

Boise

Great Falls

MONTANA

Billings

NORTH DAKOTA

Bismarck

Fargo

MINNESO

40°

CALIFORNIA

UNITED

STATES

WYOMING

SOUTH DAKOTA

Pierre

Minneapolis
St.

Sacramento

Reno

OF

Ogden

AMERICA

Sioux Falls

Oakland
San Francisco

NEVADA

UTAH

Salt Lake City
Provo

Cheyenne

COLORADO

NEBRASKA

Missouri

Sioux Cit

IOW

50°

55°

60°

120°   110°   100°

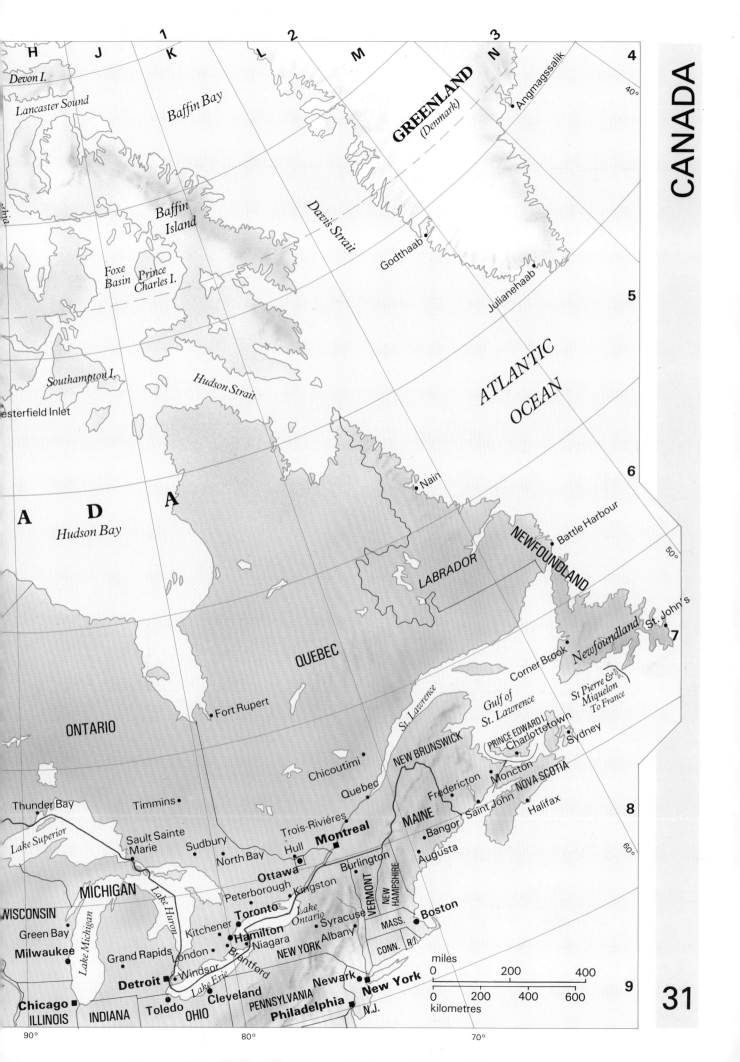

H J K 1 L 2 M N 3 4

Devon I.

Lancaster Sound

Baffin Bay

GREENLAND
(Denmark)

• Angmagssalik

40°

Baffin
Island

Davis Strait

Foxe
Basin

Prince
Charles I.

• Godthaab

5

Southampton I.

Hudson Strait

• Julianehaab

ATLANTIC

OCEAN

esterfield Inlet

6

A   **D**   **A**

Hudson Bay

• Nain

NEWFOUNDLAND

• Battle Harbour

50°

LABRADOR

7

QUEBEC

Newfoundland

• Corner Brook

St. John's

St Pierre &
Miquelon
To France

• Fort Rupert

Gulf of
St. Lawrence

St. Lawrence

ONTARIO

Chicoutimi •

NEW BRUNSWICK

PRINCE EDWARD I.
Charlottetown

• Sydney

Quebec •

Fredericton •

Moncton •

NOVA SCOTIA

8

Thunder Bay

Timmins •

Trois-Riviéres •

MAINE

Saint John •

Halifax •

Lake Superior

Sault Sainte
Marie

Sudbury •

North Bay •

Hull

Montreal

Bangor •

60°

Ottawa

Burlington •

Augusta •

MICHIGAN

Lake Huron

Peterborough •

Kingston •

VERMONT

NEW
HAMPSHIRE

WISCONSIN

Lake Michigan

Toronto

Lake
Ontario

Boston

Green Bay

Hamilton

Niagara

Syracuse •

MASS.

Milwaukee

Grand Rapids •

London •

Brantford

Albany •

NEW YORK

CONN.   R.I.

miles

0   200   400

Detroit

Windsor •

Lake Erie

Newark •

New York

0   200   400   600

kilometres

Chicago

Cleveland •

PENNSYLVANIA

Philadelphia

ILLINOIS   INDIANA   Toledo   OHIO   N.J.

90°   80°   70°

9

A   B   C   D   E   F

50°

BRITISH COLUMBIA

ROCKY

ALBERTA

Vancouver I.

• Saskatoon

Vancouver

• Calgary

SASKATCHEWAN   C   A

• Lethbridge

• Regina

45°

• Seattle

• Brandon

Olympia • Tacoma

Spokane

WASHINGTON

Portland ▲ *Mt St. Helens*

• Great Falls

Missouri

NORTH DAKOTA

• Salem

Helena •

MONTANA

• Bismarck

Eugene •

• Billings

OREGON

SALMON RIVER MTS.

SOUTH DAKOTA

• Boise   IDAHO

Pierre •

UNITED

Snake

40°

STATES

WYOMING

AMERICA

NEVADA

Great Salt Lake

• Ogden

• Cheyenne

NEBRASKA

• Reno

• Salt Lake City

San Francisco

• Carson City

Great Basin

• Provo

Sacramento

COLORADO

• **Denver**

Oakland

UTAH

▲ *Mt. Elbert 4399*

• Colorado Springs

San Jose

KANS

Fresno •

▲ *Mt. Whitney 4418*

Las Vegas •

Colorado

• Pueblo

Wic

35°

CALIFORNIA

Death Valley

• Bakersfield

Santa Barbara •

Grand Canyon

Colorado Plateau

• Santa Fe

Oklahoma

Los Angeles ■

San Bernardino •

Amarillo •

OKLAH

Long Beach

ARIZONA

Albuquerque

San Diego

NEW MEXICO

Wichita Falls •

Tijuana •

Phoenix

• **Mexicali**

Fort W

30°

PACIFIC

Tucson •

Abilene •

OCEAN

El Paso •

Ciudad Juárez

TEXA

Austin

Hermosillo •

Rio Grande

San Anton

25°

Gulf of California

Corpus Ch

Chihuahua •

Nuevo Laredo •

Ciudad Obregón •

Brown

MEXICO

Reynosa •

Saltillo •   ■ **Monterre**

miles

0   200   400

0   200   400   600

kilometres

120°   115°   110°   105°   100°

125°

COASTAL RANGE   CASCADE RANGE   SIERRA NEVADA   MOUNTAINS

H J K L M N

1

Fort Rupert

CANADA

ONTARIO

QUEBEC

2

innipeg

St. Lawrence

NEW BRUNSWICK

Thunder Bay

Timmins

Quebec

Fredericton

Saint John

Lake Superior

Trois-Riviéres

MAINE

Bangor

Sault Sainte Marie

Montreal

Augusta

MINNESOTA

MICHIGAN

Lake Huron

Ottawa

Burlington

3

Peterborough

Kingston

VERMONT

NEW HAMPSHIRE

Minneapolis

WISCONSIN

Toronto

New York

Worcester

Boston

ux Falls

St. Paul

Green Bay

Lake Michigan

Hamilton

Rochester

Utica

Albany

MASS.

Grand Rapids

Lake Ontario

Syracuse

Hartford

R.I. Providence

go

Madison

Lansing

Buffalo

Hudson

CONN.

oux City

IOWA

Milwaukee

Lake Erie

London

Cedar Rapids

Detroit

Cleveland

PENNSYLVANIA

Newark

New York

Des Moines

Chicago

Toledo

Youngstown

MTS.

N.J.

Davenport

Akron

Pittsburgh

Philadelphia

4

Omaha

Peoria

INDIANA

OHIO

Altoona

coln

ILLINOIS

Dayton

Columbus

Baltimore

Decatur

MARYLAND

DEL.

Springfield

Indianapolis

Cincinnati

Washington

Kansas City

Charleston

D.C.

peka

St. Louis

Louisville

WEST VIRGINIA

VIRGINIA

Norfolk

Evansville

Ohio

Lexington

Richmond

MISSOURI

KENTUCKY

APPALACHIAN

ulsa

Springfield

Winston-Salem

Greensboro

Tennessee

Nashville

Knoxville

Raleigh

Fort Smith

Mt. Mitchell

NORTH CAROLINA

rkansas

TENNESSEE

2037

Charlotte

5

Memphis

Chattanooga

ATLANTIC

OCEAN

Little Rock

SOUTH CAROLINA

70°

ARKANSAS

Birmingham

Atlanta

Columbia

Augusta

Charleston

Tuscaloosa

ALABAMA

Monroe

Columbus

Savannah

allas

Shreveport

MISSISSIPPI

Montgomery

GEORGIA

Jackson

Mobile

Jacksonville

LOUISIANA

Baton Rouge

Pensacola

Tallahassee

6

ouston

Port Arthur

New Orleans

FLORIDA

Orlando

Galveston

Gulf of Mexico

Tampa

Fort Lauderdale

Nassau

Miami

BAHAMAS

Florida Keys

7

CUBA

95° 90° 85° 80° 75°

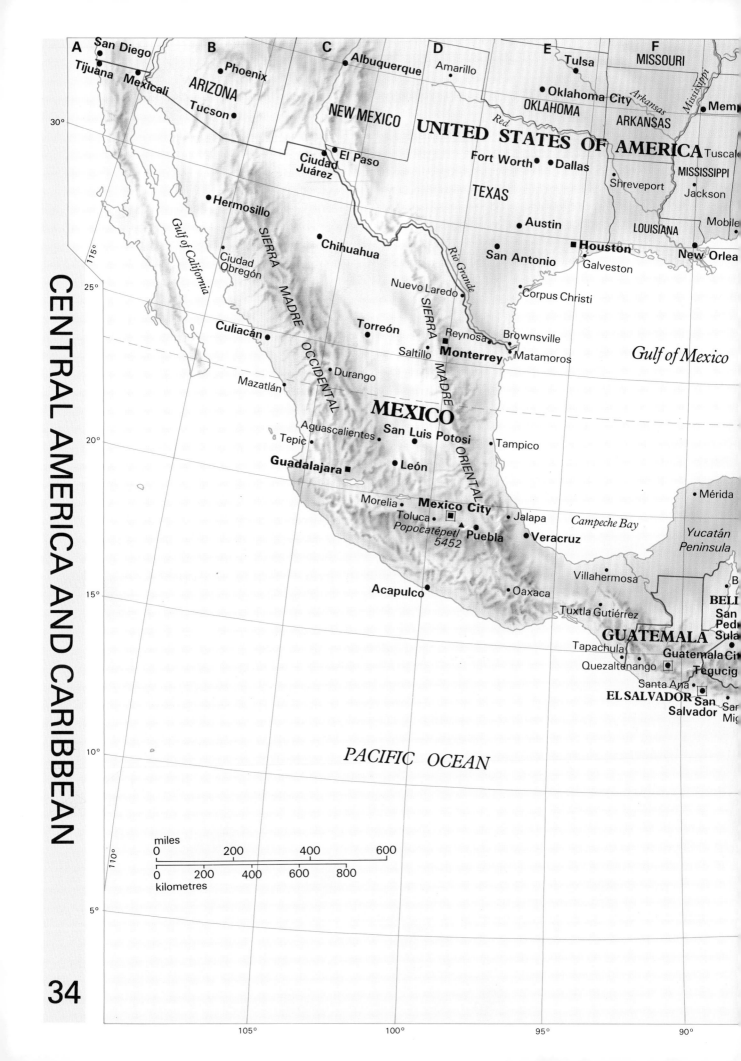

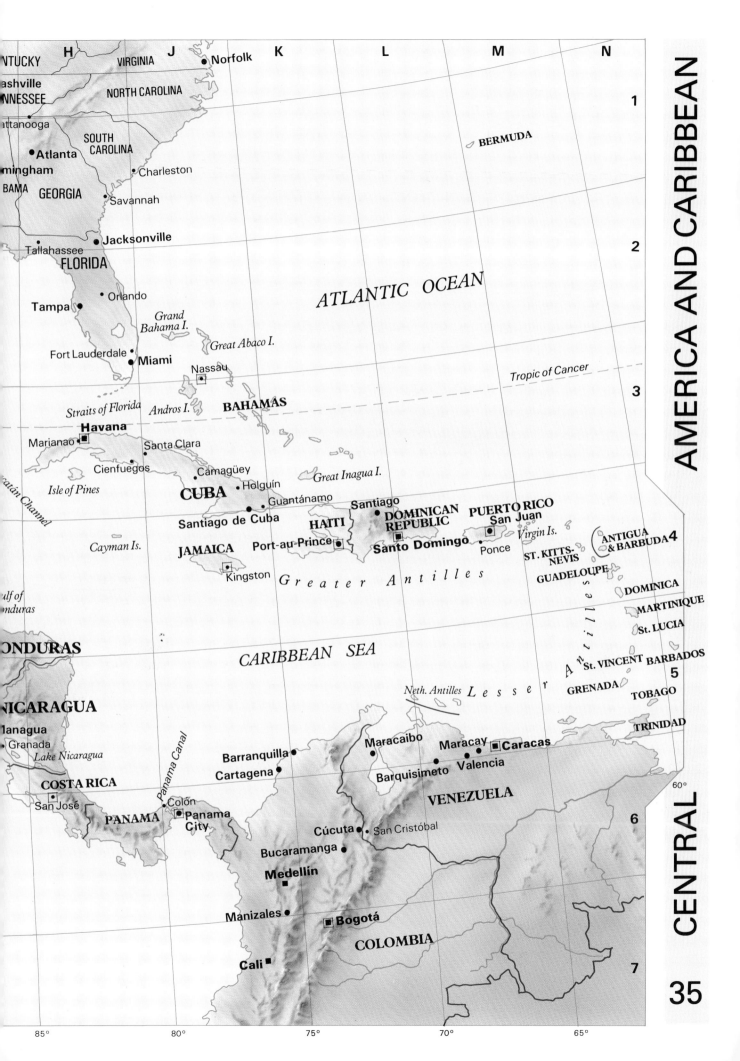

H   J   K   L   M   N

1

NTUCKY   VIRGINIA   ●Norfolk

ashville

NNESSEE   NORTH CAROLINA

attanooga

SOUTH
CAROLINA

●Atlanta

mingham

BAMA   GEORGIA   ●Charleston

●Savannah

BERMUDA

2

●Jacksonville

Tallahassee

FLORIDA

ATLANTIC OCEAN

Tampa●   ●Orlando

Grand
Bahama I.

Great Abaco I.

Fort Lauderdale   ●Miami

Tropic of Cancer

3

●Nassau

Straits of Florida   Andros I.   BAHAMAS

Havana

Marianao●

Santa Clara

●

Cienfuegos

Great Inagua I.

Isle of Pines   Camagüey

catán   CUBA   ●Holguín

Santiago   PUERTO RICO

DOMINICAN   San Juan

Channel   Guantánamo

Santiago   REPUBLIC

Santiago de Cuba   HAITI

Virgin Is.   ANTIGUA
&BARBUDA 4

Cayman Is.   Ponce

Port-au-Prince   Santo Domingo   ST. KITTS-
NEVIS

JAMAICA   DOMINICA

GUADELOUPE

●   Greater Antilles   MARTINIQUE

Kingston

ulf of   St. LUCIA

nduras   Antilles

St. VINCENT BARBADOS

NDURAS   CARIBBEAN SEA   GRENADA

Lesser   TOBAGO

NICARAGUA   Neth. Antilles   5

anagua   TRINIDAD

Granada   Maracaibo   Maracay   ■Caracas

Lake Nicaragua   Barranquilla   Valencia

Cartagena   Barquisimeto

COSTA RICA   VENEZUELA   60°

San José   Colón   PANAMA

PANAMA   Panama   Cúcuta   ●San Cristóbal   6
City

Bucaramanga

Medellín

Manizales●

Bogotá

COLOMBIA

7

Cali■

85°   80°   75°   70°   65°

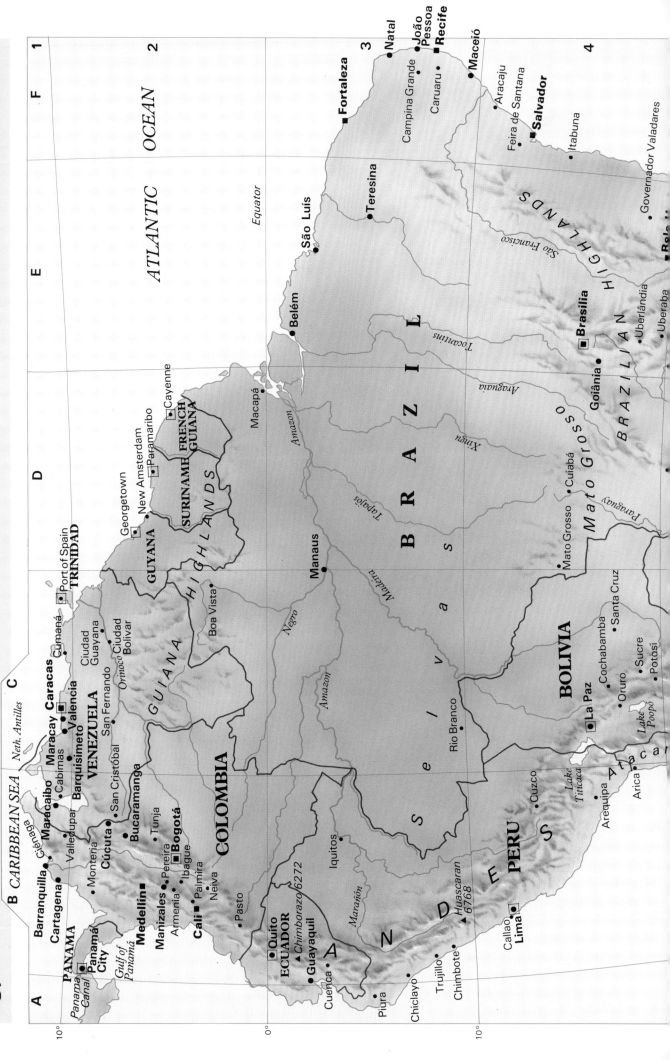

A B C D E F

1 2 3 4

10°

0°

10°

CARIBBEAN SEA

Neth. Antilles

ATLANTIC

OCEAN

Equator

PANAMA

Panama Canal

Panama City

Gulf of Panamá

Barranquilla

Cartagena

Ciénaga

Maracaibo

Cabimas

Valledupar

Montería

Cúcuta

San Cristóbal

Bucaramanga

Tunja

Medellín

Manizales

Pereira

Ibague

Armenia

Palmira

Cali

Neiva

Bogotá

COLOMBIA

Pasto

Quito

ECUADOR

Chimborazo 6272

Guayaquil

Cuenca

Piura

Chiclayo

Trujillo

Chimbote

PERU

Cuzco

Callao

Lima

Arequipa

Arica

Iquitos

Marañón

Rio Branco

Huascaran 6768

Lake Titicaca

La Paz

BOLIVIA

Oruro

Cochabamba

Sucre

Potosí

Santa Cruz

Lake Poopó

Atacama

VENEZUELA

Maracay Caracas

Cumaná

Valencia

Barquisimeto

Ciudad Guayana

Ciudad Bolívar

San Fernando

Orinoco

Port of Spain

TRINIDAD

GUYANA

Georgetown

New Amsterdam

SURINAME

Paramaribo

FRENCH GUIANA

Cayenne

GUIANA HIGHLANDS

Boa Vista

Negro

Macapá

Amazon

Manaus

Madeira

Amazon

Selvas

Rio Branco

Xingu

Tapajós

Araguaia

Tocantins

BRAZIL

BRAZILIAN HIGHLANDS

Mato Grosso

Mato Grosso

Cuiabá

Paraguay

Goiânia

Brasília

Uberlândia

Uberaba

Governador Valadares

São Francisco

Belém

São Luís

Teresina

Fortaleza

Natal

João Pessoa

Recife

Maceió

Campina Grande

Caruaru

Aracaju

Feira de Santana

Salvador

Itabuna

ANDES

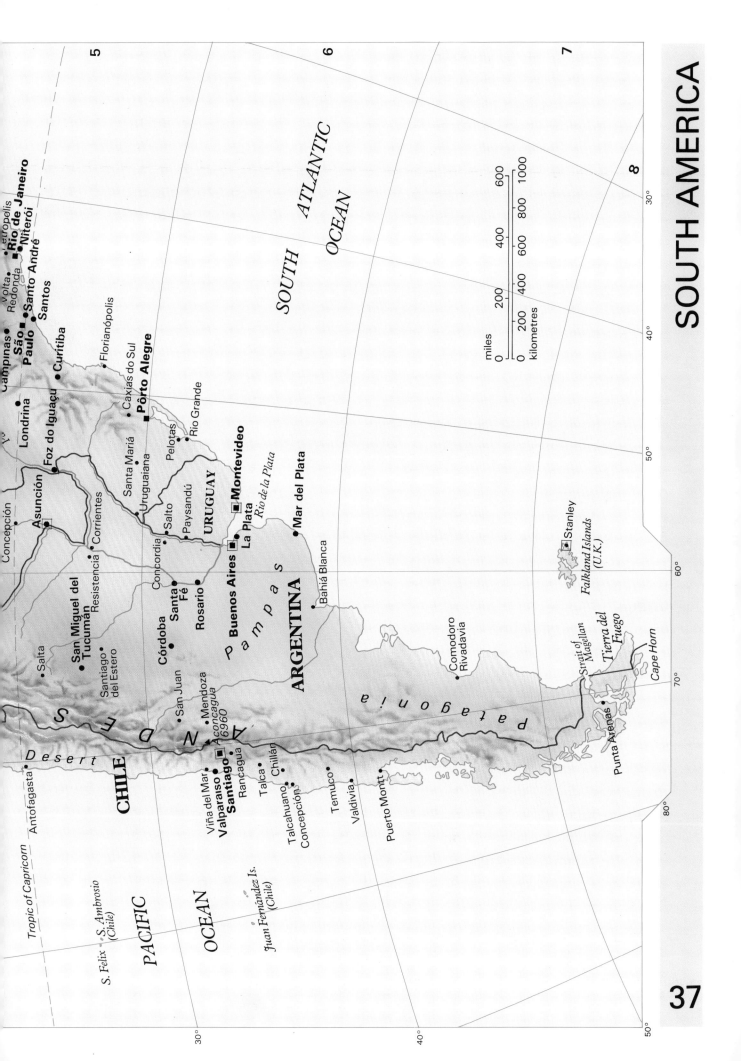

5

6

7

8

30°

40°

50°

SOUTH
ATLANTIC
OCEAN

Petrópolis
Volta
Redonda
Santo André
Rio de Janeiro
Niterói
Santos
São
Paulo
Campinas
Curitiba
Londrina
Foz do Iguaçu
Florianópolis
Caxias do Sul
Pôrto Alegre
Rio Grande
Santa Mariá
Uruguaiana
Pelotas
Salto
Paysandú
Concordia
Corrientes
Resistencia
Asunción
Concepción
San Miguel del
Tucumán
Salta
Santiago
del Estero
Córdoba
San Juan
Mendoza
Aconcagua
6960
Santa
Fé
Rosario
P Buenos Aires
La Plata
Montevideo
URUGUAY
Río de la Plata
Mar del Plata
Bahiá Blanca
P a m p a s
ARGENTINA
Viña del Mar
Valparaíso
Santiago
Rancagua
Talca
Chillán
Talcahuano
Concepción
Temuco
Valdivia
Puerto Montt
CHILE
Desert
A N D E S
P a t a g o n i a
Comodoro
Rivadavia
Strait of
Magellan
Tierra del
Fuego
Cape Horn
Punta Arenas
Stanley
Falkland Islands
(U.K.)

60°

70°

80°

Tropic of Capricorn

S. Felix
S. Ambrosio
(Chile)
Juan Fernández Is.
(Chile)

Antofagasta

PACIFIC

OCEAN

SOUTH
ATLANTIC
OCEAN

miles
0   200   400   600
0   200 400   600   800   1000
kilometres

INDONESIA

Sumba

Timor

Melville I.

TIMOR   SEA

ARNHEM LAND

• Darwin

Groote
Eyland

Gul

Katherine

• Wyndham

Birdum

KIMBERLEY
PLATEAU

BARKLY

• Derby

Hall's Creek

TABLELAND

Broome

Tennant Creek

Great Sandy Desert

NORTHERN TERRITORY

• Port Hedland

A U S T R A L I A

Dampier

MACDONNELL RANGE

HAMERSLEY
RANGE

Tropic of Capricorn

Alice Springs

Mount Newman

Simpson
Desert

BARLEE RANGE

Gibson Desert

▲*Ayers Rock*
867

Carnarvon

Lake Ey

WESTERN AUSTRALIA

MUSGRAVE RANGES

SOUTH AUSTRALIA

• Mount Magnet

Great Victoria Desert

Geraldton

• Woomera

• Kalgoorlie

N u l l a r b o r   P l a i n

Ceduna

Port Augusta

• Moora

Coolgardie

Eucla

• Northam

Eyre Pen.

Po
Pir

Perth
Fremantle
Mandurah

• Narrogin

Esperance

Great Australian Bight

Port Lincoln

Adelai

Bunbury

Spencer Gulf

Augusta

Kangaroo I.

Albany

INDIAN

OCEAN

miles
0   200   400

0   200   400   600
kilometres

115°   120°   125°   130°   135°

10°
15°
20°
25°
30°
35°
40°

A   B   C   D   E   F

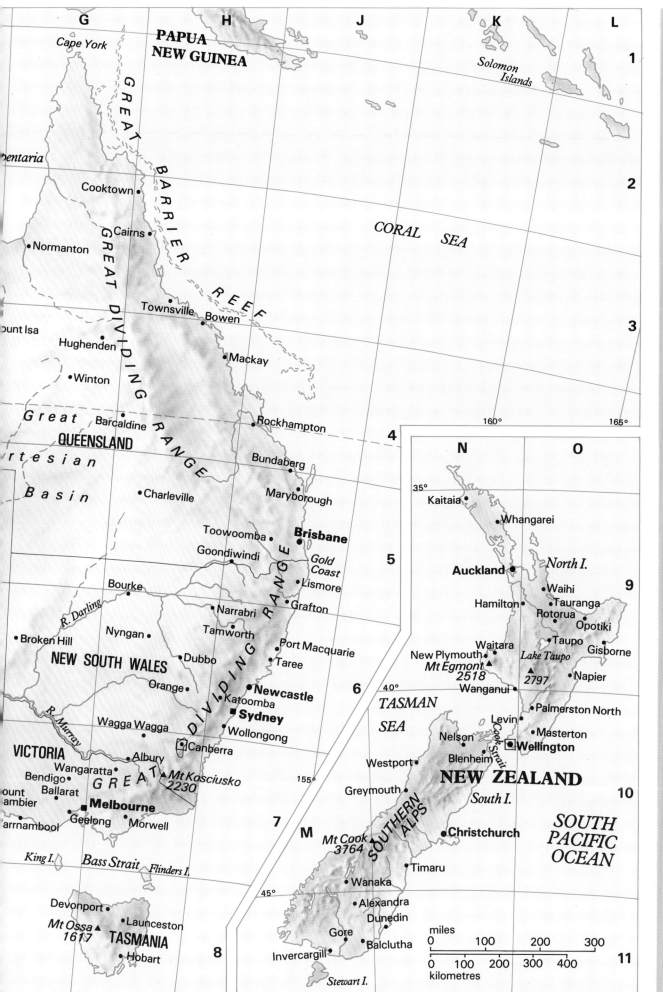

Map labels:

G H J K L
1 2 3 4 5 6 7 8 9 10 11
N O M

Cape York
PAPUA NEW GUINEA
Solomon Islands
ntaria
Cooktown
Cairns
Normanton
CORAL SEA
Townsville
Bowen
unt Isa
Hughenden
Mackay
Winton
Great
Barcaldine
Rockhampton
160°
165°
QUEENSLAND
Bundaberg
rtesian
Maryborough
Basin
Charleville
35°
Kaitaia
Whangarei
Toowoomba
Brisbane
North I.
Goondiwindi
Gold Coast
Auckland
Waihi
Lismore
Hamilton
Tauranga
Rotorua
Bourke
Narrabri
Grafton
Opotiki
R. Darling
Tamworth
Waitara
Taupo
Nyngan
Port Macquarie
New Plymouth
Lake Taupo
Gisborne
Broken Hill
Taree
Mt Egmont
2518
2797
NEW SOUTH WALES
Dubbo
Napier
Orange
Newcastle
Wanganui
Katoomba
Sydney
Palmerston North
Wagga Wagga
Wollongong
TASMAN SEA
Levin
Masterton
R. Murray
Canberra
Nelson
Wellington
VICTORIA
Albury
Westport
Blenheim
Wangaratta
GREAT
Mt Kosciusko
NEW ZEALAND
Bendigo
2230
Greymouth
South I.
ount
Ballarat
155°
SOUTH PACIFIC OCEAN
ambier
Melbourne
SOUTHERN ALPS
rrnambool
Geelong
Morwell
Mt Cook
Christchurch
King I.
Bass Strait
Flinders I.
3764
Timaru
Devonport
Wanaka
Launceston
45°
Alexandra
Mt Ossa
Dunedin
1617
TASMANIA
Gore
Balclutha
Hobart
Invercargill
Stewart I.

DIVIDING RANGE
GREAT DIVIDING RANGE
GREAT BARRIER REEF

40°

miles
0   100   200   300
0 100 200 300 400
kilometres

145°   150°   170°   175°

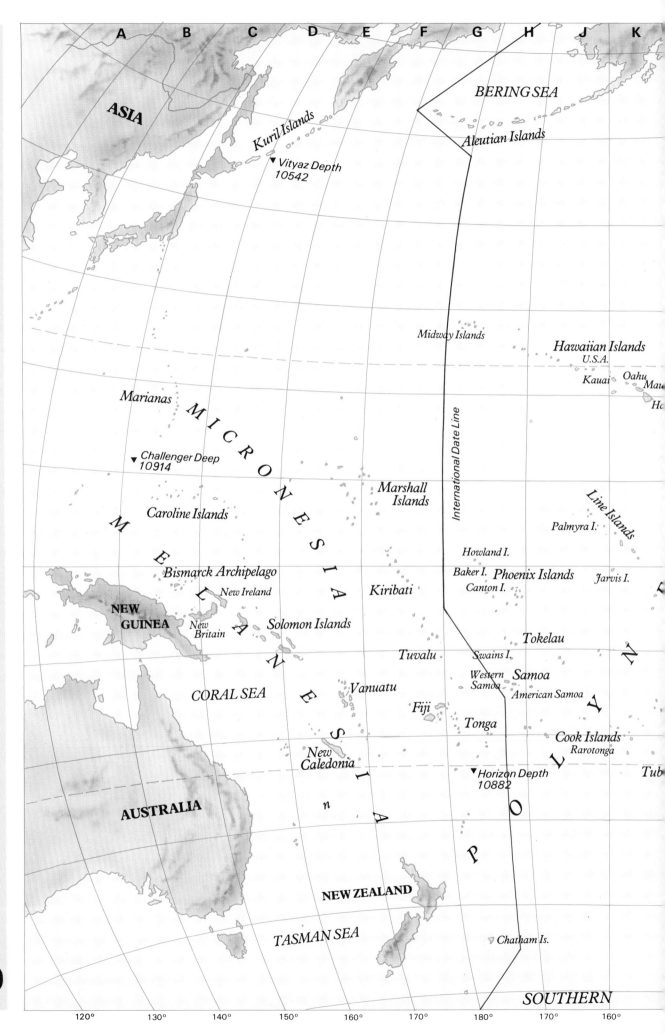

A B C D E F G H J K

ASIA

BERING SEA

Kuril Islands

Aleutian Islands

▼ Vityaz Depth
10542

Midway Islands

Hawaiian Islands
U.S.A.

Kauai Oahu Mau

Ho

Marianas

M I C R O N E S I A

International Date Line

Line Islands

▼ Challenger Deep
10914

Palmyra I.

Caroline Islands

Marshall
Islands

Howland I.

M
E
L
A
N

Bismarck Archipelago

Baker I. Phoenix Islands Jarvis I.

New Ireland

Canton I.

NEW
GUINEA

New
Britain

Kiribati

Solomon Islands

E

Tokelau

Tuvalu

Swains I.

Western
Samoa Samoa

S

Vanuatu

American Samoa

CORAL SEA

I

Fiji

Tonga

N

A

New
Caledonia

Cook Islands
Rarotonga

Tub

▼ Horizon Depth
10882

n

P
O
L
Y

AUSTRALIA

P

NEW ZEALAND

TASMAN SEA

Chatham Is.

SOUTHERN

120°   130°   140°   150°   160°   170°   180°   170°   160°

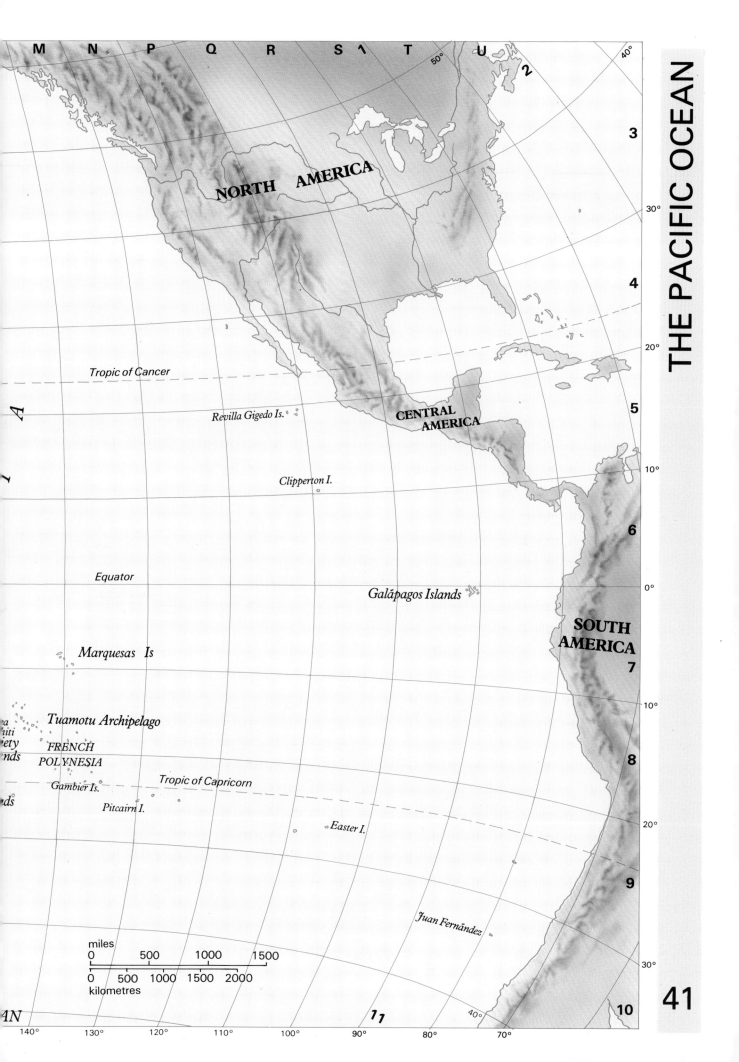

M N P Q R S 1 T U 2

50° 40°

3

NORTH AMERICA

30°

4

20°

Tropic of Cancer

A

5

Revilla Gigedo Is.

CENTRAL AMERICA

1

10°

Clipperton I.

6

Equator

Galápagos Islands

0°

SOUTH AMERICA

7

Marquesas Is

10°

Tuamotu Archipelago

a
hiti
iety
FRENCH
nds
POLYNESIA

8

Gambier Is.   *Tropic of Capricorn*

nds

Pitcairn I.

20°

Easter I.

9

Juan Fernández

30°

miles
0   500   1000   1500

0   500   1000 1500 2000
kilometres

AN

1 1

40°

10

140°   130°   120°   110°   100°   90°   80°   70°

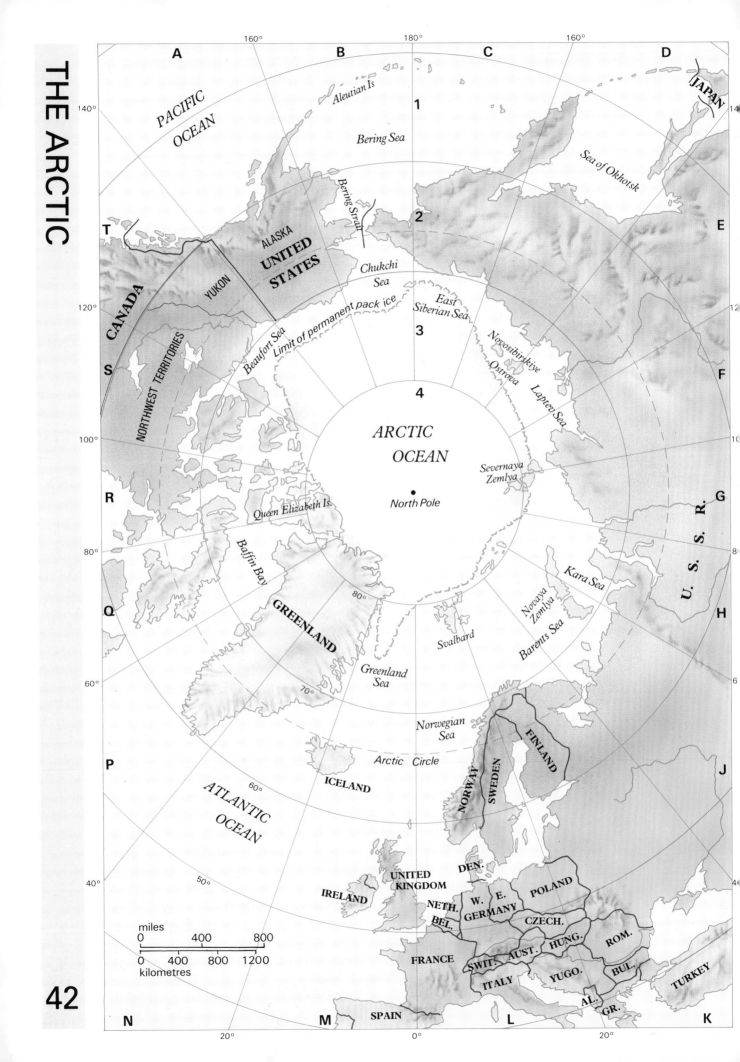

PACIFIC OCEAN

A   160°   B   180°   C   160°   D

140°

1

Aleutian Is

Bering Sea

Sea of Okhotsk

JAPAN

T

E

140°

ALASKA
UNITED
STATES

Bering Strait

2

Chukchi
Sea

East
Siberian Sea

Novosibirskiye
Ostrova

Laptev Sea

CANADA

YUKON

120°

Beaufort Sea

Limit of permanent pack ice

3

F

120°

S

NORTHWEST TERRITORIES

4

ARCTIC
OCEAN

Severnaya
Zemlya

100°

R

Queen Elizabeth Is.

North Pole

80°

Baffin Bay

GREENLAND

80°

Kara Sea

U. S. S. R.

G

Q

Novaya
Zemlya

H

Svalbard

Barents Sea

60°

70°

Greenland
Sea

Norwegian
Sea

60°

P

Arctic Circle

ICELAND

ATLANTIC
OCEAN

60°

NORWAY

SWEDEN

FINLAND

J

40°

50°

DEN.

UNITED
KINGDOM

POLAND

40°

IRELAND

NETH.

W.
GERMANY

E.

CZECH.

miles
0   400   800

BEL.

AUST.

HUNG.

ROM.

0   400   800   1200
kilometres

FRANCE

SWIT.

ITALY

YUGO.

BUL.

TURKEY

AL.

42

N   20°   M   SPAIN   0°   L   GR.   20°   K

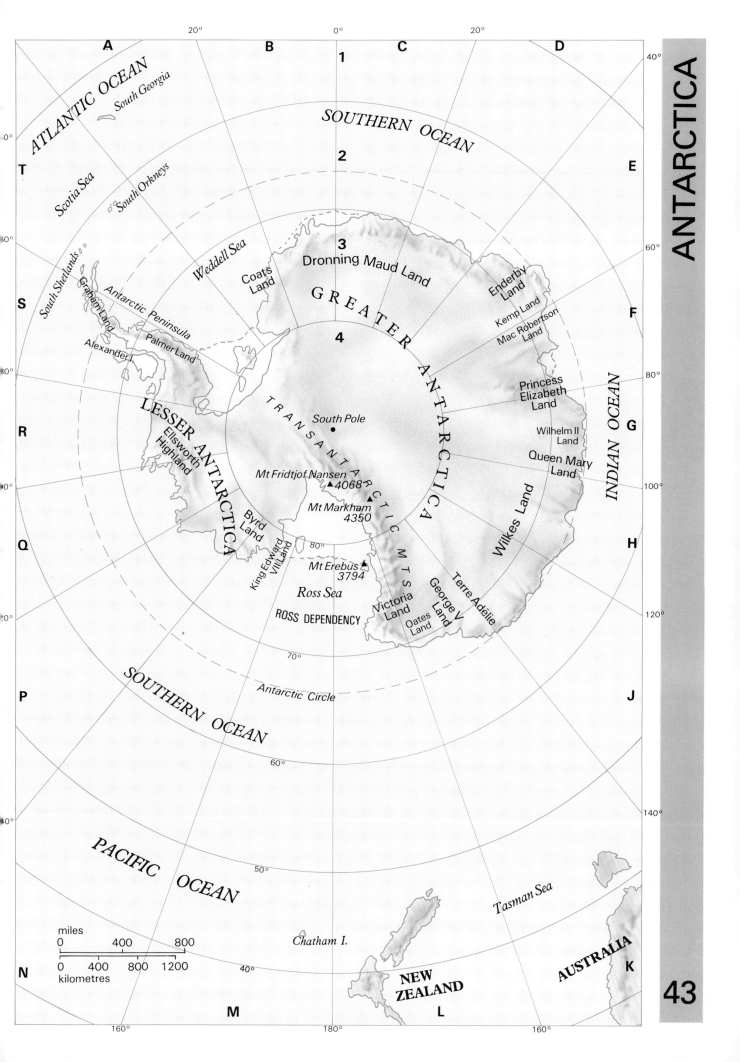

ATLANTIC OCEAN
South Georgia

SOUTHERN OCEAN

Scotia Sea

South Orkneys

Weddell Sea

Coats Land

Dronning Maud Land

Enderby Land

Kemp Land

Mac Robertson Land

GREATER ANTARCTICA

South Shetlands

Graham Land

Antarctic Peninsula

Palmer Land

Alexander I.

Princess Elizabeth Land

Wilhelm II Land

LESSER ANTARCTICA

Ellsworth Highland

TRANSANTARCTIC

South Pole

Queen Mary Land

INDIAN OCEAN

Byrd Land

Mt Fridtjof Nansen ▲4068

Mt Markham 4350

MTS

Wilkes Land

King Edward VII Land

Mt Erebus ▲ 3794

Ross Sea

ROSS DEPENDENCY

Victoria Land

George V Land

Terre Adélie

Oates Land

SOUTHERN OCEAN

Antarctic Circle

PACIFIC OCEAN

Tasman Sea

miles
0   400   800

0   400   800   1200
kilometres

Chatham I.

NEW ZEALAND

AUSTRALIA

A   B   C   D   E   F   G   H   J   K   L   M   N   P   Q   R   S   T

1   2   3   4

20°   0°   20°   40°   60°   80°   100°   120°   140°   160°   180°   160°   0°

0°   60°   80°   70°   60°   50°   40°

INDEX TO OUR WORLD

INDEX TO FLAGS

INDEX
TO
FLAGS

INDEX TO MAPS

Dore, Mt. 11 F4
Dortmund 14 B3
Douai 11 F1
Douala 29 E4
Doubs 14 B5
Douglas 6 C2
Douro 12 B2
Dover 7 J5
Downpatrick 9 F2
Drakensberg 28 N10
Drammen 13 F7
Dresden 14 E3
Drogheda 9 E3
Dronning Maud Land 43 C3
Dubai 21 G4
Dubbo 39 H6
Dubica 16 F2
Dublin 9 E3
Dubrovnik 16 G3
Dudley 6 E4
Duero 12 E2
Duisburg 14 B3
Dumbarton 8 D5
Dumfries 8 E5
Dunbar 8 F5
Dundalk 9 E2
Dundee 8 F4
Dunedin 39 N11
Dunfermaline 8 E4
Dungarvan 9 D4
Dunkirk 11 F1
Dun Laoghaire 9 E3
Durance 11 G5
Durango 34 D3
Durban 28 P9
Durham 6 F2
Durrës 17 G4
Dushanbe 18 E6
Düsseldorf 14 B3
Dvina 18 D3

E
Eastbourne 7 H6
East China Sea 25 L5
Easter I. 41 Q9
Eastern Ghats 22 D6
East Frisian Is. 14 B2
East Germany 14
East Kilbride 8 D5
East London 28 N10
East Siberian Sea 19 K2
Ebro 12 F2
Ecuador 36 B3
Edhessa 17 J4
Edinburgh 8 E5
Edirne 17 L4
Edmonton 30 E6
Egmont, Mt. 39 N9
Egypt 29 G2
Eifel 14 B3
Eigg 8 B4
Eindhoven 14 A3
El Aaiún 28 C2
Elat 20 B4
Elba 16 C3
Elbasan 17 H4
Elbe 14 E3
Elbert, Mt. 32 E4
Elblag 15 H1
Elbrus 18 D5
Elburz Mts. 21 F2
Elche 12 F3
El Ferrol 12 B1
Elgin 8 E3
El Gîza 20 B3
Elgon, Mt. 29 H4
Ellsworth Highland 43 R3

El Mahalla el Kubra 20 B3
El Mansura 20 B3
El Minya 20 B4
El Obeid 29 H3
El Paso 32 E5
El Salvador 34 G5
Elvas 12 C3
Ely 7 H4
Ems 14 B2
Ende 27 F7
Enderby Land 43 E2
Engels 18 D4
England 7
English Channel 7 D7
Enna 16 E6
Ennis 9 C4
Enniskillen 9 D2
Enschede 14 B2
Entebbe 29 H4
Enugu 29 E4
Equator 41 M6
Equatorial Guinea 29 E4
Erbil 20 D2
Erciyas, Mt. 20 C2
Erebus, Mt. 43 L3
Erfurt 14 D3
Erie, Lake 33 K3
Eriskay 8 A3
Erzurum 20 D2
Esbjerg 13 E7
Eskilstuna 13 G7
Eskimo Point 30 G4
Eskisehir 20 B2
Esperance 38 C6
Essen 14 B3
Ethiopia 29 J4
Ethiopian Highlands 29 H3
Etna, Mt. 16 E6
Euboea 17 J5
Eucla 38 D6
Eugene 32 B3
Euphrates 20 D2
Europe 4
European Plain 5 F2
Evansville 33 J4
Everest, Mt. 23 F3
Evora 12 C3
Exeter 7 D6
Exmoor 7 D5
Eyre, Lake 38 F5
Eyre Peninsula 38 F6

F
Fairbanks 30 B4
Fair Isle 8 G1
Faisalabad 22 C2
Faizabad (Afghanistan) 21 K2
Faizabad (India) 23 E3
Fakfak 27 H6
Falkirk 8 E5
Falkland Is. 37 D8
Falmouth 7 B6
Faradofay 29 J7
Farah 21 H3
Fargo 33 G2
Faro 12 C4
Faroe Is. 13 D5
Fársala 17 J5
Fauske 13 G5
Feira de Santana 36 F4
Felixtowe 7 J5
Fens, The 6 H4
Ferrara 16 C2
Fez 28 D1
Ffestiniog 6 D3
Fiji 40 G8
Finland 13

Finland, Gulf of 13 J7
Firth of Clyde 8 D5
Firth of Forth 8 F4
Firth of Lorn 8 C4
Firth of Tay 8 F4
Fishguard 7 C5
Flamborough Head 6 G2
Flensburg 14 C1
Flinders I. 39 H7
Flinders Range 38 F6
Florence 16 C3
Flores 26 F7
Flores Sea 26 E7
Florianópolis 37 E5
Florida 35 H2
Florida, Straits of 35 H3
Foggia 16 E4
Folkestone 7 J5
Foochow 25 J5
Forfar 8 F4
Forli 16 D2
Fortaleza 36 F3
Fort Lauderdale 35 H2
Fort Portal 29 H4
Fort Reliance 30 F4
Fort Rupert 31 J6
Fort St. John 30 D5
Fort Smith 33 H4
Fort William 8 C4
Fort Worth 32 G5
Fougères 10 D2
Foxe Basin 31 J3
Foyle, Lough 9 D1
Foz do Iguaçu 37 D5
France 10
Frankfurt (E. Germany) 15 F2
Frankfurt (W. Germany) 14 C3
Franz Josef Land 18 D1
Fraserburgh 8 G3
Fredericton 31 K7
Fredrikshavn 13 F7
Freetown 28 C4
Freiburg 14 B5
Fremantle 38 B6
French Guiana 36 D2
Fresno 32 C4
Fribourg 11 H3
Fröya 13 E6
Frunze 18 E5
Fuji 25 N3
Fukuoka 25 M4
Fulda 14 C3
Fürth 14 D4
Fushun 25 K2
Fusin 25 K2

G
Gabon 29 F5
Gaborone 28 N8
Gainsborough 6 G3
Galapagos Is. 41 R7
Galashiels 8 F5
Galati 17 L2
Galdhöpiggen 13 E6
Galle 22 E7
Gallipoli 17 L4
Gällivare 13 H5
Galveston 33 H6
Galway 9 B3
Galway Bay 9 B3
Gambia 28 C3
Gambier Is. 41 M9
Ganges 23 E3
Gao 28 E3
Garda, Lake 16 C2
Garonne 10 E5
Gascony, Gulf of 10 C5

Gateshead 6 F2
Gauhati 23 G3
Gävle 13 G6
Gdańsk 15 H1
Gdańsk, Gulf of 15 H1
Gdynia 15 H1
Gebel Katherina 20 B4
Geelong 39 G7
Gelsenkirchen 14 B3
Gemas 26 B5
General Santos 27 G4
Geneva 11 H3
Geneva, Lake 11 H3
Genoa 16 B2
Genoa, Gulf of 16 B2
Gent 11 F1
George Town 26 B4
Georgetown 36 D2
George V Land 43 K3
Georgia 33 K5
Gera 14 E3
Geraldton 38 A5
Gerlachovka 15 J4
Germiston 28 N9
Ghana 28 D4
Ghardaïa 28 E1
Ghazni 21 J3
Gibraltar 12 D4
Gibraltar, Strait of 12 D5
Gibson Desert 38 C4
Gijón 12 D1
Gilgit 22 C1
Gillingham 7 H5
Gironde 10 D4
Girvan 8 D5
Gisborne 39 O9
Giurgiu 17 K3
Glåma 13 F6
Glasgow 8 D5
Glen More 8 D3
Glenrothes 8 E4
Glogów 15 F3
Gloucester 7 E5
Gmünd 15 F4
Gobi Desert 19 G5
Godavari 22 E5
Godthaab 31 L4
Goiânia 36 E4
Gold Coast 39 J5
Gomel 18 C4
Gondar 29 H3
Good Hope, Cape of 28 L10
Goole 6 G3
Gore 39 M11
Gorgan 21 F2
Gorizia 16 D2
Gorki 18 D4
Görlitz 15 F3
Göteborg 13 F7
Gotland 13 G7
Governador Valadares 36 E4
Grafton 39 J5
Graham Land 43 S2
Grahamstown 28 N10
Grampian Mts. 8 D4
Granada (Nicaragua) 35 G5
Granada (Spain) 12 E4
Grand Bahama I. 35 J2
Grand Canyon 32 D4
Grand Rapids 33 J3
Grantham 6 G4
Grantown-on-Spey 8 E3
Gravesend 7 H5
Grays 7 H5
Graz 15 F5
Great Abaco I. 35 J2

Kalinin 18 C4
Kaliningrad 18 C4
Kalisz 15 H3
Kalmar 13 G7
Kamchatka Peninsula 19 J4
Kampala 29 H4
Kampot 26 B3
Kampuchea 26 C3
Kananga 29 G5
Kanazawa 25 N3
Kanchenjunga 23 F3
Kandahar 21 J3
Kandalaksha 13 K5
Kangaroo I. 38 F7
Kankan 28 D3
Kano 29 E3
Kanpur 22 E3
Kansas 32 G4
Kansas City 33 H4
Kansk 19 F4
Kaohsiung 25 K6
Kapfenberg 16 E1
Karachi 22 B4
Karaganda 18 E5
Karakoram Pass 22 D1
Karakoram Range 22 D1
Kara Sea 18 E2
Karbala 20 D3
Karl Marx Stadt 14 E3
Karlovac 16 E2
Karlovy Vary 14 E3
Karlskrona 13 G7
Karlsruhe 14 C4
Karlstad 13 F7
Karnobat 17 L3
Karpáthos 17 L7
Kasai 29 F5
Kasama 29 H6
Kassala 20 C6
Kassel 14 C3
Kastoria 17 H4
Katherine 38 E2
Katmandu 23 E3
Katoomba 39 J6
Katowice 15 H3
Katsina 29 E3
Kauai 40 K4
Kaunas 15 K1
Kawasaki 25 N3
Kayseri 20 C2
Kazan 18 D4
Kéa 17 K6
Kebnekaise 13 G5
Kecskemet 15 H5
Kediri 26 D7
Kefallinía 17 H5
Keflavik 13 A3
Keighley 6 F3
Keith 8 F3
Kékes 15 J5
Kells 9 E3
Kemerovo 18 F4
Kemi 13 H5
Kemi R. 13 J5
Kemp Land 43 E3
Kempten 14 D5
Kendal 6 E2
Kendari 27 F6
Kenitra 28 D1
Kenmare 9 B5
Kenora 30 G7
Kentucky 33 J4
Kenya 29 H4
Kenya, Mt. 29 H4
Kerintji 26 B6
Kerman 21 G3
Kesan 17 L4

Keswick 6 D2
Kettering 7 G4
Khabarovsk 19 H5
Khaburah 21 G5
Khairpur 22 B3
Khalkis 17 J5
Kharkov 18 C4
Khartoum 20 B6
Khartoum North 20 B6
Kherson 18 C5
Khíos 17 L5
Khorramabad 20 E3
Khorramshahr 20 E3
Khulna 23 F4
Khyber Pass 21 K3
Kiamusze 25 M1
Kiev 18 C4
Kigali 29 G5
Kikinda 17 H2
Kikwit 29 F5
Kildare 9 E3
Kilimanjaro, Mt. 29 H5
Kilkee 9 B4
Kilkenny 9 D4
Kilkis 17 J4
Killarney 9 B4
Kilmarnock 8 D5
Kilrush 9 B4
Kimberley 28 M9
Kimberley Plateau 38 D3
King Edward VII Land 43 N3
King I. 39 G7
King's Lynn 6 H4
Kingston 35 J4
Kingston upon Hull 6 G3
Kinshasa 29 F5
Kirgiz Steppe 5 J3
Kiribati 40 G7
Kirin 25 L2
Kirkcaldy 8 E4
Kirkenes 13 K5
Kirklareli 17 L4
Kirkuk 20 D2
Kirkwall 8 F2
Kirov 18 D4
Kirovabad 20 E1
Kiruna 13 H5
Kisangani 29 G4
Kishinev 18 C5
Kisumu 29 H5
Kitakyushu 25 M4
Kitchener 31 H8
Kíthira 17 J6
Kíthnos 17 K6
Kitwe 29 G6
Kizil 20 C2
Klagenfurt 15 F5
Klaipeda 13 H7
Knoxville 33 K4
Kobe 25 N4
Koblenz 14 B3
Kola 13 K5
Kolding 13 E7
Kolguyev 18 D3
Kolhapur 22 C5
Kolobrzeg 15 F1
Kolwezi 29 G6
Kolyma Range 19 K3
Komotini 17 K4
Komsomolets 19 F1
Komsomolsk-na-Amur 19 H4
Konya 20 B2
Kopet Range 21 G2
Korce 17 H4
Kos 17 L6
Kosciusko, Mt. 39 H7
Kosice 15 J4

Kostroma 18 D4
Kostrzyn 15 F2
Koszalin 15 G1
Kota 22 D3
Kota Baharu 26 B4
Kota Kinabalu 26 E4
Kotelnyy 19 H2
Kotka 13 J6
Kotor 17 G3
Kowloon 25 H6
Kragujevac 17 H2
Krakow 15 H3
Krasnodar 18 C5
Krasnoyarsk 19 F4
Kratie 26 C3
Krems 15 F4
Kristiansand 13 E7
Krivoy Rog 18 C5
Kroonstad 28 N9
Krugersdorp 28 N9
Kuala Lumpur 26 B5
Kuching 26 D5
Kudat 26 E4
Kufstein 16 D1
Kumamoto 25 M4
Kumasi 28 D4
Kunlun Shan 23 F1
Kunming 24 F5
Kuopio 13 J6
Kupang 27 F8
Kurgan 18 E4
Kuril Is. 19 J5
Kurnool 22 D5
Kursk 18 C4
Kustanay 18 E4
Kuwait 20 E4
Kuybyshev 18 D4
Kwangju 25 L3
Kweiyang 24 G5
Kyle of Lochalsh 8 C3
Kyluchevskaya 19 K4
Kyoto 25 N3
Kyushu 25 M4

L
Labrador 31 K6
La Coruña 12 B1
Ladysmith 28 M10
Lagos (Nigeria) 28 E4
Lagos (Portugal) 12 B4
Lahore 22 C2
Lahti 13 J6
Lairg 8 D2
Lake District 6 D2
Lakselv 13 H4
Lakshadweep Is. 22 C6
Lamía 17 J5
Lancaster 6 E2
Lancaster Sound 31 H2
Lanchow 24 F3
Landeck 16 C1
Land's End 7 B6
Lansing 33 K3
Laoag 26 F2
Lao Cai 26 B1
Laos 26 C2
La Paz 36 C4
Lapland 13 H5
La Plata 37 D6
La Plata, Rio de 37 D6
Laptev Sea 19 H2
Lárisa 17 J5
Larne 9 F2
La Roshe-sur-Yon 10 D3
Las Palmas 28 C2
La Spezia 16 B2
Las Vegas 32 C4

Latakia 20 C2
Lauchhammer 14 E3
Launceston 39 H8
Lausanne 11 H3
Leamington Spa 7 F4
Lebanon 20 C3
Leeds 6 F3
Legnica 15 G3
Leh 22 D2
Le Havre 10 E2
Leicester 6 F4
Leipzig 14 E3
Le Mans 10 E3
Lena 19 H3
Leninabad 18 E5
Leningrad 18 C4
Lens 11 F1
Leoben 15 F5
León 34 D3
Léon 12 D1
Le Puy 11 F4
Lérida 12 G2
Lerwick 8 A1
Les Ecrins 11 H4
Leskovac 17 H3
Lesotho 28 N9
Lesser Antilles 35 M5
Lesser Sundra Is. 26 E7
Lésvos 17 L5
Leszno 15 G3
Lethbridge 30 E7
Lewis 8 B2
Lexington 33 K4
Leyte 27 G3
Lhasa 23 G3
Liaoyuan 25 L2
Liberec 15 F3
Liberia 28 D4
Libreville 29 E4
Libya 29 F2
Libyan Desert 29 G2
Liechtenstein 14 C5
Liège 11 G1
Lienz 16 D1
Liepaja 13 H7
Liffey 9 E3
Ligurian Sea 16 B3
Likasi 29 G6
Lille 11 F1
Lillehammer 13 F6
Lilongwe 29 H6
Lima 36 B4
Limerick 9 C4
Límnos 17 K5
Limoges 10 E4
Limpopo 28 N8
Linares 12 E3
Lincoln 6 G3
Lindos 17 M6
Line Is. 40 J6
Linköping 13 G7
Linz 15 F4
Lions, Gulf of 11 G5
Lipari Is. 16 E5
Lisbon 12 B3
Lisburn 9 E2
Lismore 39 J5
Little Rock 33 H5
Liuchow 25 G6
Liverpool 6 E3
Livingstone 29 G6
Livorno 16 C3
Lizard Point 7 B7
Ljubljana 16 E1
Llandrindod Wells 7 D4
Llandudno 6 D3
Llanelli 7 C5

Lobito 29 F6
Locarno 16 B2
Lódź 15 H3
Lofoten Is. 13 F5
Logan, Mt. 30 B4
Logroño 12 E1
Loire 10 D3
Lom 17 J3
Lombok 26 E7
Lomé 28 E4
Lomond, Loch 8 D4
Lomza 15 K2
London (Canada) 31 H8
London (England) 7 G5
Londonderry 9 D2
Londrina 37 D5
Long Beach 32 C5
Longford 9 D3
Lorient 10 C3
Los Angeles 32 C5
Lot 10 E4
Loughborough 6 F4
Louisiana 33 H5
Louis Trichardt 28 N8
Louisville 33 J4
Lourdes 10 D5
Lower Lough Erne 9 D2
Lowestoft 6 J4
Loyang 25 H4
Luanda 29 F5
Luang Prabang 26 B2
Luanshya 29 G6
Lubango 29 F6
Lübeck 14 D2
Lublin 15 K3
Lubumbashi 29 G6
Lucknow 22 E3
Ludhiana 22 D2
Lugo 12 C1
Lugoj 17 H2
Lule 13 H5
Luleå 13 H5
Luleburgaz 17 L4
Lurgan 9 E2
Lusaka 29 G6
Lü-ta 25 K3
Luton 7 G5
Luxembourg 14 B4
Luxor 20 B4
Luzern 11 J3
Luzon 27 F2
Luzon Strait 27 F2
Lvov 18 C5
Lyon 11 G4

M
Maas 14 A3
Maastricht 14 A3
Macao 25 H6
Macapá 36 D2
McClintock Channel 30 F2
McClure Strait 30 E2
Macdonnell Range 38 E4
Maceió 36 F3
Machilipatnam 22 E5
Mackay 39 H4
Mackenzie 30 D4
Mackenzie Mts. 30 C4
McKinley, Mt. 30 A4
Macomer 16 B4
Mâcon 11 G3
Mac Robertson Land 43 F2
Madagascar 29 J7
Madeira 28 C1
Madeira R. 36 C3
Madison 33 J3
Madras 22 E6

Madrid 12 E2
Madurai 22 D7
Mafikeng 28 N9
Magadan 19 J4
Magdeburg 14 D2
Magellan, Strait of 37 C8
Maggiore, Lake 16 B2
Magnitogorsk 18 D4
Mahajanga 29 J6
Maidstone 7 H5
Maiduguri 29 F3
Main 14 D3
Maine 33 N2
Mainz 14 C4
Majene 26 E6
Majorca 12 H3
Makassar Strait 26 E6
Makhachkala 18 D5
Malabo 29 E4
Malacca, Strait of 26 B5
Málaga 12 D4
Malang 26 D7
Malange 29 F5
Mälaren, Lake 13 G7
Malatya 20 C2
Malawi 29 H6
Malawi, Lake 29 H6
Malaysia 26
Malbork 15 H1
Malegaon 22 C4
Mali 28 D3
Mallow 9 C4
Malmö 13 F7
Malta 16 E7
Manado 27 F5
Managua 35 G5
Manama 21 F4
Manaus 36 D3
Manchester 6 E3
Mandala Peak 27 K6
Mandalay 23 H4
Mandurah 38 B6
Mangalia 17 M3
Mangalore 22 C6
Manila 26 F3
Manisa 17 L5
Manitoba 30 G5
Manizales 36 B2
Mansfield 6 F3
Maoke Range 27 J6
Maputo 28 P9
Maracaibo 36 B1
Maracay 36 C1
Maragheh 20 E2
Marañón 36 B3
Maras 20 C2
Marathon 17 J5
Marbella 12 D4
Mar del Plata 37 D6
Mardin 20 D2
Margate 7 J5
Marianao 35 H3
Marianas 40 D5
Maribor 16 E1
Maritsa 17 K3
Marmara, Sea of 17 M4
Marmaris 17 M6
Marne 11 F2
Marquesas Is. 41 M7
Marrakesh 28 D1
Marseille 11 G5
Marshall Is. 40 G6
Martaban, Gulf of 23 H5
Martinique 35 M5
Maryborough 39 J5
Maryland 33 L4
Masan 25 L3

Maseru 28 N9
Mashhad 21 G2
Mask, Lough 9 B3
Massachusetts 33 M3
Massawa 29 H3
Massif Central 11 F4
Masterton 39 O10
Masvingo 29 H7
Matadi 29 F5
Matamoros 34 E2
Mathura 22 D3
Mato Grosso 36 D4
Matruh 20 A3
Matsuyama 25 M4
Matterhorn 16 A2
Maui 40 K4
Mauritania 28 C3
Mazar-i-Sharif 21 J2
Mazatlán 34 C3
Mbabane 28 P9
Mbandaka 29 F4
Mbuju Mayi 29 G5
Mecca 20 C5
Medan 26 A5
Medellín 36 B2
Medina 20 C5
Meerut 22 D3
Meissen 14 E3
Meknès 28 D1
Mekong 26 B2
Melbourne 39 G7
Melville I. (Australia) 38 E2
Melville I. (Canada) 30 E1
Memmingen 14 D5
Memphis 33 J4
Mendi 27 K7
Mendoza 37 C6
Merauke 27 K7
Mergui Archipelago 23 H6
Mérida (Mexico) 34 G3
Mérida (Spain) 12 C3
Mersin 20 B2
Merthyr Tydfil 7 D5
Meseta 4 C4
Mesolóngion 17 H5
Messina 16 E5
Metković 16 F3
Metz 11 H2
Meuse 11 G1
Mexicali 34 A1
Mexico 34
Mexico, Gulf of 34 F2
Mexico City 34 E4
Mezenc, Mt. 11 G4
Miami 35 H2
Michigan 33 J2
Michigan, Lake 33 J3
Micronesia 40
Middlesbrough 6 F2
Midway Is. 40 H4
Midye 17 M4
Milan 16 B2
Milâs 17 L6
Milford Haven 7 B5
Milos 17 K6
Milton Keynes 7 G5
Milwaukee 33 J3
Mindanao 27 G4
Mindoro 26 F3
Minneapolis 33 H2
Minnesota 33 H2
Minorca 12 J3
Minsk 18 C4
Miquelon 31 L7
Mirzapur 23 E3
Miskolc 15 J4
Misool 27 H6

Mississippi 33 J5
Mississippi R. 33 H3
Missouri 33 H4
Missouri R. 32 E2
Misurata 29 F1
Mitchell, Mt. 33 K4
Mitilíni 17 L5
Miyazaki 25 M4
Mobile 33 J5
Moçambique 29 J6
Modena 16 C2
Moffat 8 E5
Mogadishu 29 J4
Moluccas 27 G6
Mombasa 29 H5
Monaco 16 A3
Monaghan 9 E2
Mönchen-Gladbach 14 B3
Moncton 31 K7
Monghyr 23 F3
Mongolia 19 G5
Mongu 29 G6
Monroe 33 H5
Monrovia 28 C4
Mons 11 F1
Montana 32 E2
Montargis 11 F3
Montauban 10 E5
Montélimar 11 G4
Monteria 36 B2
Monterrey 34 D2
Montevideo 37 D6
Montgomery 33 J5
Montluçon 11 F3
Montpellier 11 F5
Montreal 31 J7
Montreux 11 H3
Montrose 8 F4
Monza 16 B2
Moora 38 B6
Moorea 41 L8
Moose Jaw 30 F6
Mora 13 F6
Moradabad 22 D3
Moray Firth 8 E3
Morecambe 6 E2
Morelia 34 D4
Morlaix 10 C2
Morocco 28 D1
Morwell 39 H7
Moscow 18 C4
Mosel 14 B4
Mossel Bay 28 M10
Mostar 16 F3
Mosul 20 D2
Motala 13 F7
Motherwell 8 E5
Moulmein 23 H5
Mount Gambier 39 G7
Mount Isa 39 F4
Mount Magnet 38 B5
Mount Newman 38 B4
Mozambique 29 H6
Mozambique Channel 29 J6
Mukachevo 15 K4
Mukalla 20 E7
Mulhacén 12 E4
Mulhouse 11 H3
Mull 8 C4
Multan 22 C2
Munich 14 D4
Münster 14 B3
Murcia 12 F4
Mures 17 J1
Murmansk 18 C3
Murray 39 G7
Murud 26 E5

Muscat 21 G5
Musgrave Ranges 38 E5
Mutankiang 25 L2
Mutare 29 H6
Muzaffarpur 23 F3
Mwanza 29 H5
Myingyan 23 H4
Myitkyina 23 H3
Mysore 22 D6
My Tho 26 C3

N
Naas 9 E3
Nagasaki 25 L4
Nagercoil 22 D7
Nagoya 25 N3
Nagpur 22 D4
Nagykanizsa 15 G5
Naha 25 L5
Nain 31 K5
Nairn 8 E3
Nairobi 29 H5
Nakhodka 19 H5
Nakhon Ratchasima 26 B2
Nakhon Sawan 26 B2
Nakuru 29 H5
Namibia 28 L9
Namib Desert 28 L8
Nampula 29 H6
Namur 11 G1
Nanchang 25 J5
Nancy 11 H2
Nanda Devi 22 E2
Nander 22 D5
Nanga Parbat 22 C1
Nanking 25 J4
Nanning 24 G6
Nantes 10 D3
Napier 39 O9
Naples 16 E4
Narayanganj 23 G4
Narbonne 11 F5
Narodnaya 18 E3
Narrabri 39 H6
Narrogin 38 B6
Narva 13 J7
Narvik 13 G5
Nashville 33 J4
Nasik 22 C5
Nassau 35 J2
Nasser, Lake 20 B5
Natal 36 F3
Návpaktos 17 H5
Návplion 17 J6
Náxos 17 K6
N'Djamena 29 F3
Ndola 29 G6
Neagh, Lough 9 E2
Nebraska 32 G3
Negoiu 17 K2
Negro 36 C3
Negros 27 F4
Neisse 15 F3
Neiva 36 B2
Nellore 22 E6
Nelson 39 N10
Nenagh 9 C4
Nene 6 G4
Nepal 23 E3
Ness, Loch 8 D3
Netherlands 14
Neubrandenburg 14 E2
Neuchâtel 11 H3
Neuchâtel, Lac de 11 H3
Neumünster 14 C1
Neusiedler, Lake 15 G5
Nevada 32 C3

Nevis 35 M4
New Amsterdam 36 D2
Newark 33 M3
Newark-on-Trent 6 G3
New Britain 40 E7
New Brunswick 31 K7
New Caledonia 40 F9
Newcastle 39 J6
Newcastle-under-Lyme 6 E3
Newcastle-upon-Tyne 6 F1
New Delhi 22 D3
Newfoundland 31 L7
New Guinea 40 D7
New Hampshire 33 M3
New Ireland 40 E7
New Jersey 33 M3
New Mexico 32 E5
New Orleans 33 J6
New Plymouth 39 N9
Newport (England) 7 F6
Newport (Wales) 7 E5
Newquay 7 B6
New Ross 9 E4
Newry 9 E2
New Siberian Is. 19 J2
New South Wales 39 H6
Newton 6 D4
Newton Stewart 8 D6
Newtownabbey 9 F2
New York 33 M3
New Zealand 39 N10
Nha Trang 26 C3
Niagara Falls 31 J8
Niamey 28 E3
Nias 26 A5
Nicaragua 35 H5
Nicaragua, Lake 35 G5
Nice 11 H5
Nicobar Is. 23 G7
Nicosia 20 B2
Niger 29 F3
Niger, R. 28 D3
Nigeria 29 E4
Niigata 25 N3
Nikšić 17 G3
Nile 20 B4
Nîmes 11 G5
Ningpo 25 K5
Nis 17 H3
Niterói 37 E5
Nizhniy Tagil 18 D4
Noirmoutier, Île de 10 C3
Nordvik 19 G2
Norfolk 33 L4
Norilsk 18 F3
Normanton 39 G3
Norrköping 13 G7
Northam 38 B6
Northampton 7 G4
North Bay 31 J7
North Cape 13 J4
North Carolina 33 L4
North Channel 6 B2
North Dakota 32 F2
North Downs 7 G5
Northern Ireland 9 E2
Northern Territory 38 E4
North I. 39 O9
North Korea 25 L2
North Pole 42
North Sea 4 D2
North Uist 8 A3
North West Highlands 8 C3
Northwest Territories 30 E4
North York Moors 6 F2
Norway 13
Norwegian Sea 4 C2

Norwich 6 J4
Nottingham 6 F4
Nouadhibou 28 C2
Nouakchott 28 C3
Novara 16 B2
Nova Scotia 31 K8
Novaya Siberia 19 J2
Novaya Zemlya 18 D2
Novgorod 18 C4
Novi Sad 17 G2
Novokuznetsk 18 F4
Novosibirsk 18 F4
Novosibirskiye 42 D3
Nubian Desert 20 B5
Nuevo Laredo 34 E2
Nullarbor Plain 38 D6
Nuremberg 14 D4
Nyngan 39 H6

O
Oahu 40 K4
Oakland 32 B4
Oates Land 43 K3
Oaxaca 34 E4
Ob 18 F4
Oban 8 C4
Obi 27 G6
October Revolution I. 19 F2
Odda 13 E6
Odense 13 F7
Oder 15 F2
Odessa 18 C5
Offenbach 14 C3
Offenburg 14 B4
Ogbomosho 28 jE4
Ogden 32 D3
Ogulin 16 E2
Ohio 33 K3
Ohio, R 33 J4
Ohrid 17 H4
Ohridsko, Lake 17 H4
Okayama 25 M4
Okehampton 7 D6
Okha 19 J4
Okhotsk, Sea of 19 J4
Oklahoma 32 G4
Oklahoma City 32 G4
Öland 13 G7
Olbia 16 B4
Oldenburg 14 C2
Oldham 6 E3
Oléron, Île d' 10 D4
Olomouc 15 G4
Olsztyn 15 J2
Olympia 32 B2
Olympus, Mt. 17 J4
Omagh 9 D2
Omaha 33 G3
Oman 21 G5
Oman, Gulf of 21 G5
Omdurman 20 B6
Omsk 18 E4
Onega, Lake 18 C3
Onitsha 28 E4
Ontario 31 H6
Ontario, Lake 33 L3
Oporto 12 B2
Opotiki 39 O9
Oradea 17 H1
Oran 28 D1
Orange 39 H6
Orange R. 28 L9
Ordzhonikidze 18 D5
Orebro 13 G7
Oregon 32 B3
Orel 18 C4
Ore Mts. 14 E3

Orenburg 18 D4
Orense 12 C1
Orinoco 36 C2
Oristano 16 B5
Orkney Is. 8 F1
Orlando 35 H2
Orléans 11 E3
Orsk 18 D4
Oruro 36 C4
Osaka 25 N4
Osh 18 E5
Oshogbo 28 E4
Osijek 17 G2
Oslo 13 F7
Osnabrück 14 C2
Osorno 12 D1
Ossa, Mt. 39 H8
Ostend 11 F1
Östersund 13 F6
Ostrava 15 H4
Otranto 17 G4
Otranto, Strait of 17 G4
Ottawa 31 J7
Ouagadougou 28 D3
Oudtshoorn 28 M10
Ouessant, Île d' 10 B2
Oujda 28 D1
Oulu 13 J5
Ouse 6 F2
Outer Hebrides 8 A3
Oviedo 12 D1
Oxford 7 F5

P
Paarl 28 L10
Padang 26 B6
Padua 16 C2
Paisley 8 D5
Pakanbaru 26 B5
Pakistan 22 B3
Pakse 26 C2
Palawan 26 E4
Palembang 26 B6
Palencia 12 D1
Palermo 16 D5
Palma 12 H3
Palmer Land 43 S3
Palmerston North 39 O10
Palmira 36 B2
Pampas 37 C6
Pamplona 12 F1
Panama 35 H6
Panamá, Gulf of 36 B2
Panama Canal 35 J6
Panama City 35 J6
Panay 27 F3
Pantelleria 16 C6
Paoki 24 G4
Paoting 25 J3
Paotow 25 G2
Papua, Gulf of 27 K7
Papua New Guinea 27 K7
Paraguay 37 D5
Paraguay R. 36 D4
Paramaribo 36 D2
Paraná 37 D5
Paris 11 F2
Parkano 13 H6
Parma 16 C2
Pasto 36 B2
Patagonia 37 C7
Patiala 22 D2
Patna 23 F3
Pátras 17 H5
Pau 10 D5
Pavlodar 18 E4
Paysandú 37 D6

Samothráki 17 K4
Samsun 20 C1
Sana 20 D6
San Ambrosio 37 B5
San Antonio 32 G6
San Bernardino 32 C5
San Cristóbal 36 B2
San Diego 32 C5
Sandringham 6 H4
San Felix 37 A5
San Fernando 36 C2
San Francisco 32 B4
San Jose (Costa Rica) 35 H6
San Jose (USA) 32 B4
San Juan (Argentina) 37 C6
San Juan (Puerto Rico) 35 L4
San Luis Potosi 34 D3
San Marino 16 D3
San Miguel 34 G5
San Miguel del Tucumán 37 C5
San Pablo 27 F3
San Pedro Sula 34 G4
San Salvador 34 G5
San Sebastián 12 F1
Santa Ana 34 G5
Santa Barbara 32 C5
Santa Clara 35 J3
Santa Cruz 36 C4
Santa Fe 32 E4
Santa Fé 37 C6
Santa María 37 D5
Santander 12 E1
Santarém 12 B3
Santiago (Chile) 37 B6
Santiago (Dom. Rep.) 35 K4
Santiago de Compostela 12 B1
Santiago de Cuba 35 J3
Santiago del Estero 37 C5
Santo André 37 E5
Santo Domingo 35 L4
Santos 37 E5
São Francisco 36 E4
São José do Rio Prêto 36 E5
São Luís 36 E3
Saône 11 G3
São Paulo 37 E5
São Tomé 28 E4
Sapporo 25 O2
Sarajevo 17 G3
Saratov 18 D4
Sarawak 26 D5
Sardinia 16 B4
Sargodha 22 C2
Sark 10 C2
Saskatchewan 30 F6
Saskatchewan R. 30 F6
Saskatoon 30 F6
Sássari 16 B4
Satu Mare 17 J1
Saudi Arabia 20
Sault Sainte Marie 31 H7
Sava 16 F2
Savannah 33 K5
Scafell Pike 6 D2
Scarborough 6 G2
Schwerin 14 D2
Scilly Is. 7 A7
Scotia Sea 43 T1
Scotland 8
Scunthorpe 6 G3
Seattle 32 B2
Segovia 12 D2
Seine 11 F2
Sekondi-Takoradi 28 D4
Selkirk Mts. 30 E6
Selvas 36 C3
Semarang 26 D7

Semipalatinsk 18 F4
Sendai 25 O3
Sénégal 28 C3
Senegal 28 C3
Senja 13 G5
Sennar 20 B7
Seoul 25 L3
Serov 18 E4
Sérrai 17 J4
Setúbal 12 B3
Severn 6 D4
Severnaya Zemlya 19 F2
Seville 12 D4
Seward 30 B4
Seydhisfjördhur 13 C2
Sfax 29 F1
Shah Fuladi 21 J3
Shahjahanpur 22 D3
Shanghai 25 K4
Shannon 9 D3
Shantar Is. 19 H4
Shaoyang 25 H5
Sharjah 21 G4
Sheffield 6 F3
Shëngjin 17 G4
Shenyang 25 K2
Shetland Is. 8 A1
Shihkiachwang 25 H3
Shikoku 25 M4
Shilka 19 G4
Shin, Loch 8 D2
Shiraz 21 F4
Shizuoka 25 N4
Shkodër 17 G3
Shkodër, Lake 17 G3
Sholapur 22 D5
Shreveport 33 H5
Shrewsbury 6 E4
Shwebo 23 H4
Sialkot 22 C2
Siam, Gulf of 26 B3
Sian 25 G4
Siangtan 25 H5
Siauliai 13 H7
Siberut 26 A6
Sibu 26 D5
Sicily 16 D6
Sidi-bel-Abbès 28 D1
Siedlce 15 K2
Siegen 14 C3
Sierra Leone 28 C4
Sierra Madre Occidental 34 C2
Sierra Madre Oriental 34 E3
Sierra Morena 12 D3
Sierra Nevada (Spain) 12 E4
Sierra Nevada (USA) 32 C4
Siglufjördhur 13 B1
Siirt 20 D2
Si Kiang 25 H6
Silgarhi 22 E3
Silistra 17 L2
Simeulue 26 A5
Simferopol' 18 C5
Simpson Desert 38 F4
Sines 12 B4
Singapore 26 B5
Sining 24 F3
Sinop 20 C1
Sintang 26 D5
Sioux City 33 G3
Sioux Falls 33 G3
Siracusa 16 E6
Sisophon 26 B3
Sittwe 23 G4
Sivas 20 C2
Skagerrak 13 E7
Skagway 30 C5

Skegness 6 H3
Skellefteå 13 H6
Skíros 17 K5
Skopje 17 H3
Skye 8 B3
Slagelse 13 F7
Sligo 9 C2
Slough 7 G5
Smöla 13 E6
Smolyan 17 K4
Snaefell 6 C2
Snake 32 D3
Snåsa 13 F6
Snowdon 6 C3
Society Is. 41 L8
Sofia 17 J3
Sogne Fjord 13 E6
Söke 17 L6
Sokoto 28 E3
Solomon Is. 40 E7
Solway Firth 6 D2
Somali Republic 29 J4
Sombor 17 G2
Somerset I. 30 G2
Somme 11 F1
Songkhla 26 B4
Soochow 25 K4
Söröya 13 H4
Sortavala 13 K6
South Africa 28 M10
South America 36
Southampton 7 F6
Southampton I. 31 H4
South Atlantic Ocean 37 F6
South Australia 38 E5
South Carolina 33 K5
South China Sea 26 D3
South Dakota 32 F3
South Downs 7 G6
Southend 7 H5
Southern Alps 39 N10
Southern Ocean 43
Southern Uplands 8 D5
South Georgia 43 A1
South I. 39 N10
South Korea 25 L3
South Orkneys 43 T2
South Pacific Ocean 39 O10
South Pole 43
Southport 6 D3
South Shetlands 43 T2
South Shields 6 F2
South Uist 8 A3
South Yemen 20 E6
Soweto 28 N9
Spain 12
Spalding 6 G4
Spencer Gulf 38 F7
Spey 8 E3
Spittal 16 D1
Split 16 F3
Spokane 32 C2
Spree 15 F3
Springfield (Ill., USA) 33 J4
Springfield (Mo., USA) 33 H4
Springs 28 N9
Spurn Head 6 H3
Sri Lanka 22 E7
Srinagar 22 C2
Stafford 6 E4
Stanley 37 D8
Stara Zagora 17 K3
Stargard 16 E1
Stavanger 13 E7
Stavropol' 18 D5
Stewart I. 39 M11
Stirling 8 E4

Stockholm 13 G7
Stockport 6 E3
Stockton-on-Tees 6 F2
Stoke-on-Trent 6 E3
Stonehaven 8 F4
Stonehenge 7 F5
Stornoway 8 B2
Strabane 9 D2
Strait of Dover 7 J6
Stralsund 14 E1
Stranraer 8 D6
Strasbourg 11 H2
Stratford-upon-Avon 7 F4
Stromeferry 8 C3
Stroud 7 E5
Stuttgart 14 C4
Suakin 20 C6
Subotica 17 G1
Suchow 25 J4
Sucre 36 C4
Sudan 20 B6
Sudbury 31 H7
Sudeten Mts. 15 G3
Suez 20 B3
Suez, Gulf of 20 B4
Suez Canal 20 B3
Sukkur 22 B3
Sulaiman Range 22 B3
Sulawesi 26 F6
Sulu Sea 26 E4
Sumatra 26 B6
Sumba 26 E7
Sumbawa 26 E7
Sumy 18 C4
Sunderland 6 F2
Sundsvall 13 G6
Superior, Lake 33 J2
Surabaya 26 D7
Surakarta 26 D7
Surat 22 C4
Surinam 36 D2
Svalbard 42 L3
Sverdlovsk 18 E4
Swains I. 40 H8
Swansea 7 D5
Swatow 25 J6
Swaziland 28 P9
Sweden 13
Swindon 7 F5
Switzerland 11
Sydney (Australia) 39 J6
Sydney (Canada) 31 K7
Syktyvkar 18 D3
Syracuse 33 L3
Syr Darya 18 E5
Syria 20 C2
Syrian Desert 20 C3
Szczecin 15 F2
Szeged 15 J5
Szombathely 15 G5

T
Tabora 29 H5
Tabriz 20 E2
Tabuk 20 C4
Tacoma 32 B2
Taegu 25 L3
Taejon 25 L3
Taganrog 18 C5
Tagus 12 C3
Tahiti 41 L8
Taichung 25 K6
Tainan 25 K6
Taipei 25 K5
Taiwan 25 K6
Taiyuan 25 H3
Taizz 20 D7

Tajrish 21 F2
Talaud Is. 27 G5
Talca 37 B6
Talcahuano 37 B6
Tallahassee 35 H1
Tallinn 18 C4
Tamale 28 D4
Tamar 7 C6
Tambov 18 D4
Tampa 35 H2
Tampere 13 H6
Tampico 34 E3
Tamworth (Australia) 39 J6
Tamworth (England) 6 F4
Tana 13 J5
Tanga 29 H5
Tanganyika, Lake 29 G5
Tangier 28 D1
Tangshan 25 J3
Tanimbar Is. 27 H7
Tanjungkarang 26 C7
Tanta 20 B3
Tanzania 29 H5
Tapachula 34 F5
Tapajós 36 D3
Tarancón 12 E2
Táranto 16 F4
Tarbert 8 B3
Tarbes 10 E5
Taree 39 J6
Tarnow 15 J3
Tarragona 12 G2
Tarrasa 12 G2
Tashkent 18 E5
Tasmania 39 H8
Tasman Sea 39 N10
Tat-ung 25 H2
Taunton 7 D5
Taupo 39 O9
Taupo, Lake 39 O9
Tauranga 39 O9
Taurus Mts. 20 B2
Tavoy 23 H6
Tawau 26 E5
Tay 8 E4
Tay, Loch 8 D4
Taymyr Peninsula 18 F2
Tbilisi 18 D5
Tees 6 F2
Tegucigalpa 34 G5
Tehran 21 F2
Teifi 7 C4
Tekirdag 17 L4
Tel-Aviv-Yafo 20 B3
Telford 6 E4
Temirtau 18 E4
Temuco 37 B6
Tennant Creek 38 E3
Tennessee 33 J4
Tennessee R. 33 J4
Tepic 34 D3
Teresina 36 E3
Terni 16 D3
Terre Adélie 43 J3
Tete 29 H6
Tetuan 28 D1
Texas 32 G5
Thailand 26 B2
Thames 7 F5
Thar Desert 22 C3
Tharthar Basin 20 D3
Thásos 17 K4
Thessaloniki 17 J4
Thimbu 23 F3
Thionville 11 H2
Thíra 17 K6
Thunder Bay 31 H7

Thuringian Forest 14 D3
Thurles 9 D4
Thurso 8 E2
Tiber 16 D3
Tibesti Mts. 29 F3
Tibetan Plateau 23 F2
Tientsin 25 J3
Tierra del Fuego 37 C8
Tigris 20 D3
Tijuana 34 A1
Timaru 39 N10
Timbuktu 28 D3
Timisoara 17 H2
Timmins 31 H7
Timor 27 G7
Timor Sea 38 C2
Tínos 17 K6
Tipperary 9 C4
Tiranë 17 G4
Tiraspol 17 M1
Tiree 8 B4
Tîrgu Mures 17 K1
Tirich Mir 21 K2
Tirso 16 B4
Tiruchirapalli 22 D6
Tisza 15 J5
Titicaca, Lake 36 C4
Titograd 17 G3
Titov Veles 17 H4
Tlemcen 28 D1
Toamasina 29 J6
Toba, Lake 26 A5
Tobago 35 M5
Tobruk 29 G1
Tocantins 36 E3
Togo 28 E4
Tokelau 40 H7
Tokyo 25 N3
Tolbukhin 17 L3
Toledo (Spain) 12 D3
Toledo (USA) 33 K3
Toliara 29 J7
Toluca 34 E4
Tol'yatti 18 D4
Tomsk 18 F4
Tonga 40 H8
Tonle Sap 26 B3
Toowoomba 39 J5
Topeka 33 G4
Torbay 7 D6
Töre 13 H5
Torne 13 H5
Toronto 31 J8
Torreón 34 D2
Torres Strait 27 K8
Tortosa 12 G2
Toruń 15 H2
Toulon 11 G5
Toulouse 10 E5
Tours 10 E3
Townsville 39 H3
Tralee 9 B4
Trang 26 A4
Transantarctic Mts. 43
Transylvanian Alps 17 J2
Trápani 16 D5
Trasimeno, Lake 16 D3
Trebon 15 F4
Trent 6 G3
Trieste 16 D2
Tríkkala 17 H5
Trincomalee 22 E7
Trinidad 36 C1
Tripoli (Lebanon) 20 C3
Tripoli (Libya) 29 F1
Trivandrum 22 D7
Trois-Rivières 31 J7

Trollhättan 13 F7
Tromso 13 G5
Trondheim 13 F6
Trondheim Fjord 13 F6
Tropic of Cancer 41 M4
Tropic of Capricorn 41 N9
Troyes 11 G2
Trujillo 36 B3
Truro 7 B6
Tsinan 25 J3
Tsingtao 25 K3
Tsitsihar 25 K1
Tsumeb 29 F6
Tuamotu Archipelago 41 L8
Tubuai Is. 40 K9
Tucson 32 D5
Tula 18 C4
Tulcea 17 M2
Tulsa 33 G4
Tunbridge Wells 7 H5
Tunghwa 25 L2
Tunis 29 F1
Tunisia 29 E1
Tunja 36 B2
Turin 16 A2
Turkana, Lake 29 H4
Turkey 20 B2
Turku 13 H6
Turnu Severin 17 J2
Tuscaloosa 33 J5
Tuticorin 22 D7
Tuvalu 40 G8
Tuxtla Gutiérrez 34 F4
Tuz, Lake 20 B2
Tuzla 17 G2
Tweed 8 F5
Tyne 6 E1
Tyrrhenian Sea 16 D5
Tyumen 18 E4
Tzekung 24 F5

U
Ubangi 29 G4
Uberaba 36 E4
Uberlândia 36 E4
Ubon Ratchathani 26 B2
Udaipur 22 C4
Udine 16 D1
Udon Thani 26 B2
Ufa 18 D4
Uganda 29 H4
Ujjain 22 D4
Ujung Pandang 26 E7
Ulan Bator 19 G5
Ulan-Ude 19 G4
Ullapool 8 C3
Ulm 14 C4
Ul'yanovsk 18 D4
Ume 13 G6
Umeå 13 H6
United Arab Emirates 21 F5
United States of America 32
Upington 28 M9
Upper Lough Erne 9 D2
Uppsala 13 G7
Ural 18 D5
Ural Mts. 18 D4
Ural'sk 18 D4
Urfa 20 C2
Urmia, Lake 20 E2
Uruguaiana 37 D5
Uruguay 37 D6
Urumchi 18 F5
USSR 18
Usti nad Labem 15 F3
Ust Urt Plateau 5 J4
Utah 32 D4

Utica 33 M3
Utrecht 14 A2
Uzhgorod 15 K4

V
Vaal 28 N9
Vaasa 13 H6
Vadodara 22 C4
Vaduz 14 C5
Váh 15 H4
Valdepeñas 12 E3
Valdivia 37 B6
Valence 11 G4
Valencia (Spain) 12 F3
Valencia (Venezuela) 36 C1
Valencia, Gulf of 12 G3
Valenciennes 11 F1
Valladolid 12 D2
Valledupar 36 B1
Valletta 16 E7
Valparaíso 37 B6
Van, Lake 20 D2
Vancouver 30 D7
Vancouver I. 30 D7
Vänern, Lake 13 F7
Vannes 10 C3
Vanuatu 40 F8
Varánasi 23 E3
Vardar 17 J4
Varna 17 L3
Västerås 13 G7
Vättern, Lake 13 F7
Växjö 13 F7
Vaygach 18 D2
Vega 13 F5
Venezuela 36 C2
Venice 16 D2
Venice, Gulf of 16 D2
Veracruz 34 E4
Vercelli 16 B2
Verdun 14 A4
Vereeniging 28 N9
Verkhoyansk Range 19 H3
Vermont 33 M3
Verona 16 C2
Versailles 11 F2
Vesterålen 13 F5
Vest Fjorden 13 F5
Vesuvius 16 E4
Vettore, Monte 16 D3
Vichy 11 F3
Victoria 39 G7
Victoria, Lake 29 H5
Victoria, Mt. 23 G4
Victoria I. 30 F2
Victoria Land 43 K3
Vidin 17 J3
Vienna 15 G4
Vientiane 26 B2
Vietnam 26 C2
Vignemale, Pic de 10 D5
Vigo 12 B1
Vijayawada 22 E5
Vikna 13 F6
Villach 16 D1
Villahermosa 34 F4
Villaputzu 16 B5
Vilnius 18 C4
Viña del Mar 37 B6
Vinh 26 C2
Vinnitsa 18 C5
Virginia 33 L4
Virgin Is. 35 M4
Virovitica 16 F2
Visby 13 G7
Viscount Melville 30 F2
Vishakhapatnam 23 E5

INDEX
TO
MAPS